POLICE LAB

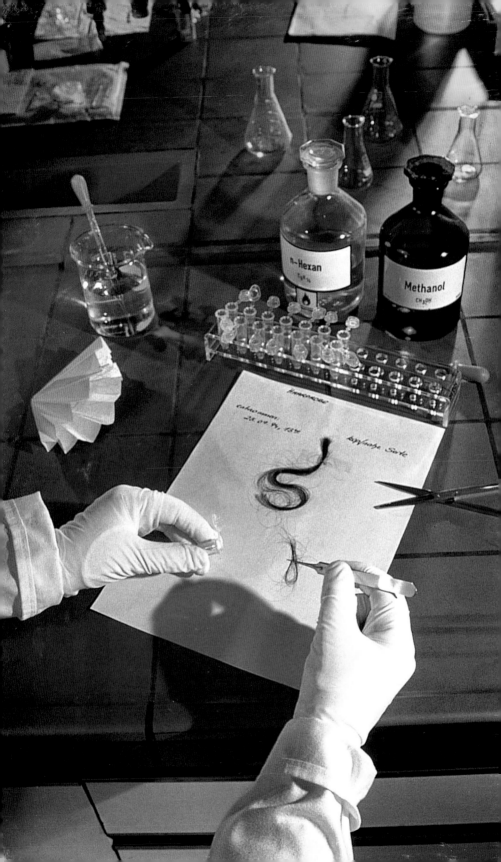

POLICE LAB

How forensic science tracks down and convicts criminals

David Owen

FIREFLY BOOKS

A FIREFLY BOOK

Published by Firefly Books Ltd., 2002

First Printing
National Library of Canada Cataloguing in Publication Data
Owen, David, 1939-
      Police lab : how forensic science tracks down and convicts criminals / David Owen.
Adapted from the author's Hidden Evidence.
Includes bibliographical references and index.
ISBN 1-55297-620-3 (bound).—ISBN 1-55297-619-X (pbk.)
      1. Forensic sciences—Juvenile literature. 2. Criminal investigation—Juvenile literature. 3. Crime—Juvenile literature.
I. Title.
HV8073.8.O94 2002   363.25   C2002-901439-5

Publisher Cataloging-in-Publication Data (U.S.)
Owen, David.
   Police lab : how forensic science tracks down and convicts criminals / David Owen.—1st ed.
[128] p. : col. ill. ; cm.
Includes bibliographical references and index.
Summary : An overview of forensic science for young adult readers that includes case studies of actual crimes
ISBN 1-55297-620-3. —ISBN 1-55297-619-X (pbk.)
1. Crime laboratories—Juvenile literature. 2. Forensic sciences—Juvenile literature. 3. Criminal investigation—Juvenile literature. (1. Crime laboratories. 2. Forensic sciences. 3. Criminal investigation.) I. Title.
363.25 21   CIP   HV8073.O94 2002

Published in Canada in 2002 by
Firefly Books Ltd.
3680 Victoria Park Avenue
Toronto, Ontario M2H 3K1

Published in the United States in 2002 by
Firefly Books (U.S.) Inc.
P.O. Box 1338, Ellicott Station
Buffalo, New York 14205

This book was designed and produced by
Quintet Publishing Limited
6 Blundell Street
London N7 7 BH

Managing Editor: Diana Steedman
Text adaptation: Victoria Sherrow
Picture Editor: Toria Leitch
Designer: James Lawrence
Creative Director: Richard Dewing
Publisher: Oliver Salzmann

Manufactured in Singapore by Universal Graphics Pte Ltd.
Printed in China

Contents

FOREWORD

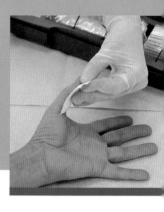

Police Lab is a fascinating book. It focuses on the development and evolution of the techniques and technologies used in forensic criminal investigation, illustrated with examples using famous or infamous cases. I have lived and worked in Los Angeles since 1952, and as I was reading, I reminisced of the days when I was involved in the investigations surrounding the deaths of Marilyn Monroe, Robert F. Kennedy, Sharon Tate, Janis Joplin, William Holden, Natalie Wood, John Belushi, and other lesser-known cases. The history of the development of the technology and advances in criminal investigation is very interesting for me—in my 50-year forensic career, I have witnessed many of the remarkable technological changes outlined in this book.

The description of the early history of forensic investigations and the discussions of some of these now-discarded theories such as the identification of criminal types by facial structure, are fascinating. Subsequent chapters are organized into selected topics covering investigation, individual identification, weapons, knives and blunt instruments, and strangulation and suffocation. Each chapter starts with an informative discussion of the various elements of specific investigative techniques, followed by factual presentation of illustrative cases, with a minimum of speculative analysis and conclusions.

Author David Owen has written for investigative-type publications since 1961. His writing credits include TV scripts, magazine articles and an encyclopedia of technology and air-accident investigation.

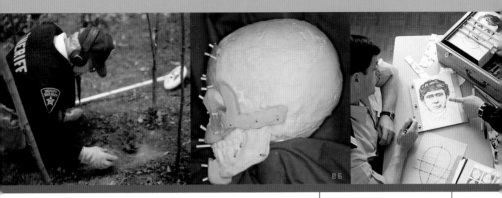

The book is strictly factual, and is easy reading for those who would like to have an introduction to the various fields of the forensic sciences, as well as for readers interested in the true facts of old and more current cases.

I found, among the cases cited, that I was either a part of the investigation or have heard and seen the scientific presentations at professional meetings, such as the annual meetings of the American Academy of Forensic Sciences (AAFS) and the National Association of Medical Examiners (NAME). I recall that at an AAFS meeting one year, I was a part of the speaker panel of the unique, annual scientific session called "The Last Word Society," where well-recognized forensic scientists are asked to review and give definitive thoughts or conclusions on well-known, unsolved cases. I was assigned to analyze the case of Jack the Ripper. The author's introduction touches upon this famous, and still unsolved, case.

I like *Police Lab* very much for its factual, non-controversial presentation of the events with only the key issues cited. It is an excellent mini-encyclopedia of widely discussed, high-profile cases. I would recommend this book for every library as an overview to the forensic science professions. *Police Lab* offers testimony to the centuries of progress in forensic medicine and sciences, and criminal investigation.

ABOVE, LEFT TO RIGHT
Preparing and cleaning the surface of a suspects thumb before fingerprinting.

Searching for clues using a metal detector.

Reconstructing the head and facial features of a victim from the dry skull.

Using an identikit to piece together the face of a criminal.

Thomas T. Noguchi, M.D.
Chief Medical Examiner-Coroner (ret.), and USC Professor Emeritus of Forensic Pathology

LOS ANGELES, CALIFORNIA

THE ORIGINS OF FORENSIC SCIENCE

A woman's body had been slashed into pieces and the floor was covered with blood. The dead woman's clothing had been burned to ashes in the fireplace.

ABOVE *The Illustrated Police News* highlighted every development.

TOP RIGHT 13 Miller's Court in Whitechapel, London where the bodies of Mary Jane Kelly and Annie Chapman—both victims of the Ripper—were found.

This is what police found in a room in London's East End one chilly morning in November 1888. That year, two other women had already been viciously murdered in this high-crime district. Witnesses reported having seen the victim, 24-year-old Mary Jane Kelly, earlier with a man who had a mustache and wore a Derby-style hat. Two witnesses said they had heard a cry of "Oh, murder!" coming from the street corner just before 4 a.m. One neighbor had heard footsteps leaving the area about two hours later.

This gruesome killing was the last in the series of savage attacks known to have been carried out by a shadowy figure nicknamed Jack the Ripper. In spite of the witness accounts and a substantial amount of forensic evidence, nobody was ever prosecuted for these crimes. For years, people tried to guess who the Ripper, suspected of murdering from five to eighteen women, might be. That question continues to puzzle writers, researchers, and police, who have speculated about the Ripper's motives and identity. More than a dozen possible suspects, including one woman, have been proposed. But the case remains unsolved.

The Ripper case illustrates both the potential and the limitations of forensic science. Modern forensic scientists have powerful tools they can use to help solve crimes. First, however, evidence must be collected and a recognizable suspect must be identified–and that requires solid, reliable police work.

In the beginning

The growth of forensic science owes much to the scientific discoveries of the sixteenth, seventeenth, and eighteenth centuries, including new kinds of microscopes. In 1590, Zacharias Jansen invented the compound microscope, using a combination of lenses to produce an image much larger than a conventional magnifying glass could provide. This technique eventually allowed investigators to scrutinize the details of a single fingerprint and compare it precisely with other prints in their files or at a crime scene.

Complex combinations of more precisely ground lenses were developed in the seventeenth century, producing far more powerful magnification. By the 1880s, optical microscopes and the comparison microscope had come into use. With new and improved microscopes, scientists examine hairs and fibers, blood samples, or scraps of cloth or other material in order to decide whether or not one sample matches another. They also can compare soil samples and paint fragments and check marks on bullets. In addition, one type of optical microscope can be used with infrared light to show whether or not documents have been tampered with.

ABOVE Cuff compound microscope, 1905, photographed in the Science Museum, London.

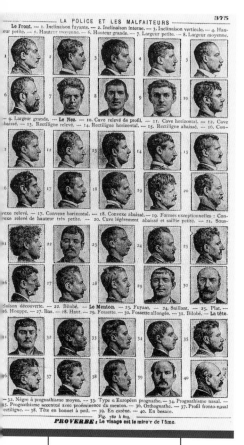

LA POLICE ET LES MALFAITEURS 375

ABOVE Police identification table.

OPPOSITE Exhibits from the 1889 Maybrick case, where Florence Maybrick was found guilty of poisoning her husband, Liverpool merchant James Maybrick, with arsenic and strychnine.

Photographs cannot lie?

Developments in photography have provided still more crime-solving techniques.

In 1724, a German inventor, Johann Heinrich Schultze, discovered the principle behind photographic film. About a century later, Frenchman Joseph Nicephore Niepce was able to produce the first "fixed" image. He worked with Louis Daguerre to develop the first photograph, called the "daguerrotype." Only one picture per exposure could be produced, however, until William Fox Talbot invented the negative, which could be used to make numerous prints.

By the 1870s, new processes enabled people to take photographs more quickly and cheaply. By then, police were using photographs routinely to record shots of evidence at crime scenes, details of victims and their injuries, and shots of suspects after they were arrested. The "Rogues' Galleries"—books of full-face and profile portraits of known criminals—aided many criminal investigations. In 1886, New York detective Thomas Byrnes had his collection of "mug shots" published in order to help the public recognize criminals who might attack or rob them.

Poison plots

For hundreds if not thousands of years, some people tried to get away with murder by using various kinds of poison. A carefully chosen poison would work slowly, secretly, and surely, without the drama and mess often produced by an openly violent crime. A knowledgeable murderer with access to certain materials might even select a poison that confused the victim and baffled investigators because it caused symptoms like heart disease, pneumonia, or other natural killers.

Modern scientific methods make it much easier to detect poisons. In 1836, English chemist James Marsh developed an accurate technique for revealing traces of arsenic. Murderers had often chosen this poison because trace amounts of arsenic already exist in the human body. But victims of arsenic poisoning have traces of the chemical throughout their bodies and it remains in the hair and bones after death. Marsh's test could reveal amounts as small as one-50th of a milligram in a sample taken from the body of someone who had died a suspicious death. The principles of his test are still in use today.

The telltale bullet

Until the 1830s, little could be done to link a particular weapon to a particular crime—unless of course the criminal was found at the scene clutching the still-smoking gun. Then, in 1835, a policeman named Henry Goddard became the first person to trace a bullet to the weapon that had fired it.

While Goddard was investigating a burglary in Southampton, England, the household's butler claimed that intruders had shot at him. Goddard found the bullet buried in the butler's bed headboard, then compared it carefully with the butler's own pistol and bullet mold. (In those days, firearm owners often molded their own bullets.) He found a raised mark on the bullet that matched a defect in the mold, proving that the shot had been fired from the butler's own weapon. Faced with the evidence, the butler admitted he had attempted to rob his employer, then fired the shot in order to divert suspicion from himself.

The science of ballistics developed further after rifled weapons and mass-produced ammunition came into use. Investigators could match bullets with the weapons that had fired them by comparing the number of grooves carved into the surface of the bullet when it was fired. The Bureau of Forensic Ballistics, founded in New York in 1923, continues to advance this increasingly sophisticated science.

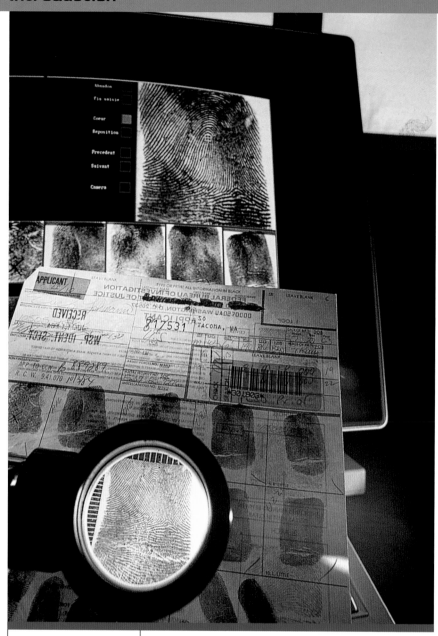

Forensic science today

For several decades, forensic evidence has been playing a larger and more critical role in a wide range of cases. Forensic science cannot find and convict a criminal unaided, but it does give detectives a powerful weapon. This weapon can be

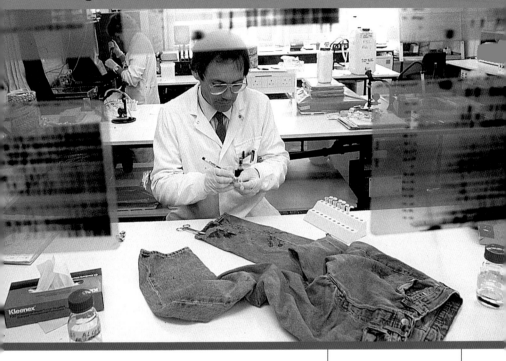

used to provide clues that help detectives to track down the criminal. It can also help them prove that a suspect was at the crime scene or committed a particular act. And sometimes it can even do both.

By using the latest methods of fingerprinting, ballistics, DNA comparison, and trace-element analysis, the modern forensic scientist can uncover facts, expose crucial details, and confirm or discount theories—all with a certainty that would have amazed previous generations. But, forensic science is not foolproof. In some cases, the evidence it isolates seems incomplete or confusing, or it is open to more than one interpretation. Experts may have different opinions about the significance of a particular finding. Moreover, techniques used to locate minute traces of a particular substance may have become so sensitive that a minor flaw in laboratory hygiene or the simplest human error could lead to mistaken conclusions. As forensic science becomes more powerful, it must be handled with even greater care if the guilty are to be convicted and the innocent cleared.

ABOVE Taking samples from blood-stained cloth to determine through **DNA** fingerprinting whether the blood was from the victim or the attacker.

THE CRIME FILE OPENS

The scene of the crime is where forensic investigators start their examinations. Here, they evaluate the first clues and form the initial impressions about the nature of the crime: What was the cause of death? Has the criminal left any identifying traces? Whose blood is that smeared on the door handle? Were any weapons hidden nearby? The first professional on the scene is usually a police officer, who closes off the site to intruders, checks bodies for signs of life and calls for medical help and other appropriate services. Extra lighting may be needed, and shelter provided over outdoor sites.

ABOVE Investigator with a bone bag at the scene of a shooting in Virginia.

Investigating officers systematically search for any evidence beyond the immediate site, and mark the exact position of anything that could possibly help their enquiry. Professional police operators take photographs and, increasingly, videotapes of the scene. If there is a dead body, it must not be disturbed until the police surgeon or forensic pathologist arrives. Officers may conduct a "fingertip search" of the whole area. They might organize this search in an expanding spiral from the center, as a grid pattern, as a strip or line search, or a search of one zone after another, depending on which approach will help them to cover the area thoroughly.

What are the searchers looking for? It may be fingerprints, shoeprints, tire tracks or prints, minute bloodstains, scratches, paint flakes, hair, fibers... the list is endless. They may lift some evidence with tape, or by dusting and brushing. When the actual bits of evidence are too small for the searchers to spot with the naked eye, they cover areas of the scene with a vacuum cleaner. Later, the contents can be checked at the forensic laboratory.

ABOVE A murder investigation in Eugene, Oregon.

Is the body still warm?

Establishing the time of death is the first priority, once the anthropologist or pathologist arrives at the crime scene. To get a realistic estimate, they usually take the internal temperature of the body, because the first measurable changes after death occur as the body begins to cool down. The internal temperature is always measured, since the outside of the body feels cold to the touch fairly soon. The temperature of the body falls from its normal level of around 98.6°F (37°C) at a rate of about 1½ to 2 degrees per hour for the first 12 hours. The rate depends on the victim's build, the amount of clothing or other insulation covering the body, and the temperature of the surroundings.

Other signs can help to pinpoint the time of death. *Rigor mortis*, a Latin term meaning "the stiffness of death," begins to take effect after death. Within about 12 hours, *rigor mortis* has fully progressed, leaving the body as stiff and unbending as a block of wood. The body can remain this rigid for anywhere between 12 and 48 hours, until further

BELOW A forensic scientist examines a body at the location of a crime.

chemical changes cause the muscles to relax again.

A condition called cadaveric spasm can occur with an especially violent death. If the victim was gripping anything at the moment of death, the object remains tightly clutched in the hand for several hours. This may provide clues about the manner of death–or even to the killer's identity.

Another indicator that can help establish the time of death is called *livor mortis*, or "the bruising of death." When the heart stops beating and the blood stops circulating, the red blood cells descend to the parts of the body in contact with the ground. This turns them a bruised color from about two hours after death.

Usually, investigators have to estimate the time of death by weighing the indications given by these different signs–internal body temperature, *rigor mortis*, *livor mortis*. More recently, Dr. John Coe, medical examiner of Hennepin County, Minneapolis, identified a different indicator. Coe's method requires taking a sample of the vitreous humor–the fluid that fills the inside of the eyeball–from the victim. This sample is tested to determine the percentage of potassium present in the liquid. This test may provide the most accurate estimate yet possible for the time of death.

Dating decay

Sometimes the body is not found until some time after death. When this happens, the processes of decay help investigators determine about how long the body has lain undiscovered.

In warmer conditions outdoors and at certain times of the year, insects can supply other clues. Flies normally lay their eggs on flesh that is still fresh, and the eggs hatch from eight to 14 hours later, depending on the temperature of the surroundings. Maggots then develop through three stages until they are full-grown. They then leave the body to develop elsewhere. By looking at these factors, forensic entomologists can guess the date of death.

Flies and plants provide evidence of time passing.

TOP The presence of fully-grown blowfly maggots and pupae shows that the body has been buried for at least 10 to 12 days.

BOTTOM Once the coffin flies expose the bones, fungus grows and woodlice establish a colony, grazing on the fungus-coated remains.

A foot out of place; a screeching tire...

Where the crime was committed by an intruder, examiners search the scene and its surroundings for footprints and possibly tire tracks. Where these are left in the soil, the forensic team will take a cast of the clearest sample. If they find footprints or tire tracks in snow, they spray the snow with a special wax to make it hard enough to take a cast.

Shoeprints are often incomplete but still can provide valuable clues about the intruder's identity, besides revealing the size of the foot. Footwear manufacturers cast soles in a vast array of patterns, which means that investigators can pinpoint a specific make and model. And, where the shoe is not new, an accurate cast can even show patterns of wear, resulting from the way the owner walks. Prints may reveal whether the intruder was walking or running, carrying a heavy weight, or even limping, all of which helps to build a fuller picture of events.

If investigators find shoeprints at the crime scene, they may extend the search to any nearby vantage points where the criminal might have laid in wait.

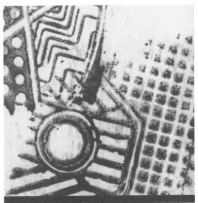

ABOVE Detail of a recorded shoeprint.

Car trouble

Earth can reveal a rich source of information for forensic scientists. For example, soil accumulates under the fenders and bodywork of vehicles. In cases where one vehicle impacts against another, lumps of soil can be dislodged, and such samples may turn up during the search of the crime scene. They can then be compared with samples taken from the soil still adhering to the underside of the suspect's vehicle. An accurate match may indicate that the vehicle was present at the crime scene.

Tire print evidence showing impression of a tread in dirt at the crime scene.

Chapter 1

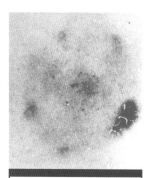

ABOVE Bite marks found on the body of Linda Peacock, murdered in Scotland in 1967, matched the individual features of her killer, Gordon Hay's teeth.

More prints may turn up behind trees or hedges, and investigators also carefully inspect any likely routes approaching the scene.

Some shoeprints cannot be preserved by plaster cast. The criminal may have stepped in wet paint or spilled blood, or left wet or muddy prints on a carpet or bare floor. In these cases, investigators take photographs to record every possible detail.

Tire tracks can be just as useful. Manufacturers and the police authorities–including the FBI–keep records of different patterns, which in turn can be traced to different tire sizes and often different makes and models of vehicles. Damage to a tire or abnormalities resulting from wear can help investigators make an even more clear-cut identification.

Cutting-edge criminals: tool and teeth marks

The tools criminals use to force entry can reveal their identity, and possibly that of their owner, simply by the marks they leave behind. When viewed under powerful magnification, even the sharpest and most standard tool, such as a chisel or a screwdriver, shows peaks and furrows along the cutting edge. The tools will then produce a distinctive pattern of scratches when used to force open a door, a window, or a desk drawer.

To preserve this valuable evidence, examiners actually remove the wood, metal, or other material that shows the tool marks. If a subsequent search turns up a tool that could have been used in the crime, examiners make a new mark on a test piece of wood or other material like the material they took from the scene. Then they use a comparison microscope to examine both marks, side-by-side, to check for the pattern of scratches.

In some cases, criminals leave more personal clues in the shape of bite marks. These may have been left on food, or there may have been a physical struggle when the victim was bitten by his or her assailant. In either case, clear marks can reveal telling evidence regarding the shape and arrangement of the criminal's teeth, information that might clear or convict a given suspect.

Air-crash investigations

For air accident investigators, the scene of impact is as crucial as the crime scene is to police. First, they draw up a record of the wreckage trail, noting the positions of any major sections of the aircraft, including engines, control surfaces, and landing gear. If these are some distance from the main wreckage, it may indicate that they became detached before the crash, and their absence may have helped to cause the disaster. Examination of the engines can show whether they were running and still delivering power at the time of the impact.

Many of the flight-deck instruments preserve the readings they showed at the time of the crash, which may help investigators to reconstruct events. In cases of fire, the pattern of burning on major components can indicate whether the fire started in the air, and possibly helped to bring down the airplane, or whether it broke out afterwards.

The tears and scratches on the airplane skin panels reveal other clues. For example, if a particular section of the skin has been torn apart, and one part shows surface scratches but the other does not, then the scratches were probably made after the panel split. If scratches can be traced on both parts of the panel, then they were made before it was torn apart.

In addition, operators of passenger aircraft are required to install increasingly sophisticated flight data recorders (F.D.Rs). Cockpit voice recorders (C.V.Rs) monitor the conversation on the flight deck on a continuously recording loop. At air traffic control centers, recordings are kept of conversations between pilots and ground controllers and of radar images of other aircraft in the area at the time.

TOP TO BOTTOM
Undamaged trees show the aircraft must have fallen horizontally.

But damage to the trees elsewhere reveals the direction of flight.

Damage to engines shows whether or not they were delivering power at the time of impact.

If scratches on the panels continue across a tear, whatever caused the scratch must have happened before impact.

JUSTICE BITES BACK

Serial killer Theodore (Ted) Bundy killed more than 40 young women in a spree spanning almost a decade. The killings began in 1969 in California and spread through Oregon and Washington and into Utah and Colorado. The murder victims all shared certain physical traits and when the various police forces compared notes on suspects they found Bundy's name kept coming up. However, nobody could prove anything more sinister than his presence in the vicinity of the crimes.

ABOVE Ted Bundy appears in court, restrained by handcuffs and a leg brace.

Bundy made his first mistake in Salt Lake City in November 1974 when he tried to abduct 18-year-old Carol DaRonch by claiming to be a plainclothes police officer. She climbed into his car, but when he produced a pair of handcuffs and tried to attack her with a crowbar, she managed to struggle free and escape. She reported the incident, but it was not until August the following year that a Salt Lake City police officer noticed a Volkswagen driver behaving suspiciously, and stopped him. A crowbar and handcuffs were found in the car, which linked the car and its owner with the attempted abduction of Carol DaRonch. She identified Bundy, and he was sentenced to 15 years' imprisonment for the attack.

Unfortunately, while being taken to Colorado to be charged with another murder in June 1977, Bundy escaped. He was recaptured after eight days, but within six months he had escaped again. In January 1978, he attacked four women in the Chi Omega sorority house at Florida State University in Tallahassee. Two of the women were killed and two were left seriously injured. An hour and a half later, Bundy attacked another woman on the same campus. She survived and was able to describe him to police.

Bundy was eventually caught in Pensacola and put on trial for the Florida murders. The crucial evidence was a bite mark on one of the victims that had been photographed and measured during the autopsy. Bundy's teeth were photographed and he was also forced to cooperate in making a cast of his bite. Some peculiarities in the arrangement of his teeth in the jaw, which exactly matched the victim's injuries, convinced the jury that he was guilty. Once Bundy had been convicted of the murders of the Florida State University students and sentenced to death, he talked about previous crimes, indicating that he could have committed between 40 and 50 murders. He was finally executed in 1989.

ABOVE Dr. Lowell Levine, chief consultant in forensic dentistry to the New York City Medical examiner, explaining the individual features of Bundy's teeth in court during the trial.

ABOVE LEFT Dentist Dr. Richard Souviron shows the jury the bitemark evidence.

POSITIVE ID

Who is the victim? This is the most fundamental question forensic scientists must tackle at the scene of the crime. If the victim died at home or was discovered by family members, friends or colleagues, then the procedure is simple enough. But if no identifying papers are found with the body, the question becomes more challenging. In some cases, bodies are not discovered until some time after death, by which time decomposition may have reduced the remains to a mere skeleton. In other cases, killers go to great lengths to destroy the victim's identity–and so the evidence of their crime–by disposing of the body as thoroughly as possible.

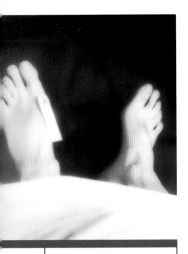

ABOVE Before undertaking an autopsy, the forensic pathologist begins by examining the body externally.

However, by using more powerful methods and equipment to analyze whatever evidence remains, forensic scientists have been able to trace a corpse's identity.

Gleaning the evidence–the autopsy

An autopsy follows a routine that begins with weighing and measuring the body and examining the clothing for any cuts or holes that may match the wounds on the body. The clothes are stored in paper bags, as are scrapings from beneath the victim's fingernails. The forensic pathologist also takes swabs for possible DNA analysis, along with saliva samples, which may indicate death by drowning or show symptoms of certain types of poisoning. Stains and dried blood are scraped to produce samples, which are stored separately for later analysis.

The pathologist then checks the body for other external symptoms of the cause of death, such as color changes associated with carbon monoxide poisoning, needle marks, or any evidence of wounds

or physical injuries. The body is washed, and the pathologist plucks and cuts samples of body hair to be stored in carefully labeled individual bags.

Next, samples of bodily fluids such as blood, urine and cerebrospinal fluid are taken. After the organs involved are removed, samples of the contents of the stomach and intestines are analyzed to find out whether or not the victim was poisoned. All these remains and samples are kept by the forensic laboratory, and the pathologist produces a detailed report on his or her findings.

ABOVE A body at the scene of a crime. Forensic scientists search for evidence that may help with identification.

TOP Blood samples being used in DNA research at Lifecodes Corporation, Valhalla, New York.

Decaying data

If the body is not discovered until some time after the killing, its condition will depend largely on the environment where it has lain or been stored. When the corpse has been kept warm and dry, the tissues have a chance to dry out before decay sets in. The body shrivels up but the structure of the face, the hair, and the rest of the individual's distinguishing features are preserved—in some cases for years.

If a body is buried in a shallow grave or left in the open, however, natural processes speed up the breakdown of the tissues. In a moist, warm environment, bacteria thrive and assist the process of decay. If the body is heavily clothed, or deeply buried in heavy soil, the lack of air circulation prevents bacteria from thriving, and that will delay the decaying process.

Total decay of the body tissue leaves only a skeleton with which to identify the victim. This job is performed by forensic anthropologists, who start by establishing whether it is a man or a women. The answer lies in the differences in the bone structure, paying special attention to pubic shape, subpubic angle and the presence of the ventral arc. To determine the victim's age, investigators examine the teeth, as well as certain bones. In the case of children, detailed changes to the teeth provide significant clues. To estimate the age of an adult, experts usually analyze the condition of the bones joined at the pubic symphysis or from the rib ends. For younger victims, they focus on the fusion of growth centers in the skeletons. Bone structure and the color and texture of the hair help to show the victim's broad racial and ethnic group.

Full skeletons can be measured to show the size of the subject. But even when a victim has been

A final check-up at the dentist

Forensic Fact

Although most people have never been fingerprinted, a large percentage of the population has dental records. A patient's dental chart can be as unique as a fingerprint. It can show where teeth have been lost through accident or extraction, and where they have been drilled, filled, or crowned, chipped, cracked or discolored. A technique called rugoscopy provides another record when a victim wore dentures. The upper plate of a set of dentures is cast from a mold taken from the upper jaw and palate, so the dentist's mold will show the unique pattern of ridges in the individual's palate.

Sometimes, a sample of dental pulp from inside the teeth can be drilled out to provide DNA material for testing (see Chapter 12).

Dental records are often used for identification purposes.

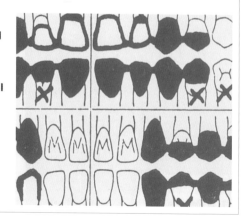

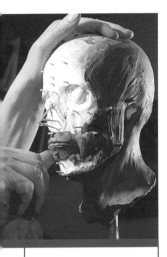

ABOVE Richard Neave, senior medical artist at Manchester University, England, demonstrating his reconstruction techniques.

BELOW The skull is then cast by hand with the final touches of hair added for authenticity.

dismembered, investigators can use formulas that help estimate the person's height. Once investigators establish the age, gender, and broad racial and ethnic groups, they can apply the formulas that will give them the most accurate data.

Facial reconstruction

During the past century, people have developed increasingly accurate ways to deduce a person's appearance when all that remains is the skull. Art meets science when forensic anthropologists use facial reconstruction to recreate the head and facial features of a victim. They begin this intricate process by making a cast of the skull. A series of holes is then drilled into the cast at certain anatomical reference points. Rods are inserted into each hole and secured so they protrude to a depth that fits the established data on the depth of soft-tissue layers at each point. Next, plastic "eyeballs" are placed in the eye sockets.

The muscular structure of the face is built up by applying layers of modeling clay to the surface of the skull until each of the rods is just covered.

The modeling begins with the neck and jaw, and continues upward to the cheeks and eyes. Superficial touches are added to give the model a more lifelike appearance. But this is the least reliable step in the reconstruction since the skeleton gives little or no information on the shape or size of the nose or the eyebrows, or the texture, length and style of the hair. Nevertheless, skilled anthropologists can achieve results that closely resemble the subject's live appearance, once the identity has been revealed and the models are compared with photographs.

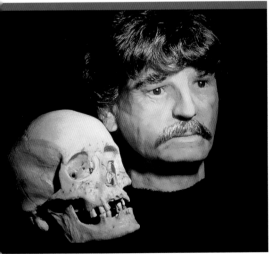

THE RUXTON BODY BAGS

Forensic science can sometimes frustrate a murderer's most determined efforts to destroy the identity of his or her victims. On September 29, 1935, police were called to search a countryside stream near Moffat in Scotland. They found four bundles containing more than 70 pieces of human flesh, some wrapped in pillowcases, some in old clothes and others in newspaper. There were two heads and one complete torso. It became clear that extreme measures had been taken to disguise the identity of the corpses. The ends of fingers had been chopped off and the ears, eyes, noses, lips, and skin had been removed from both faces.

When they searched other sites in the area, police found more body parts, including a left foot, wrapped in newspaper, and an arm a few miles away. All the body fragments were painstakingly reassembled into two badly mutilated corpses.

One of the newspapers used to wrap the remains was dated September 15 of that year. This helped investigators figure out when the bodies may have been dumped. They knew that between September 15 and the date when the body parts were found, the only time the stream had run high enough for the remains to be washed onto the bank had been before September 19.

BELOW Parts of the Morecambe paper used to wrap body parts.

Experts working on the case reported that one victim seemed to be a woman about 21 years old and the other a woman between 35 and 45 years old. Police began searching their records for anyone who had been reported missing in the days leading up to September 19. The newspaper used to wrap the remains yielded further clues. One contained an article about the crowning of the local carnival queen in Morecambe, a resort more than 100 miles to the south. Around that same time the Chief Constable pursuing the case, read in a Glasgow newspaper of a housemaid called Mary Jane Rogerson reported missing by her employer, Lancaster doctor Buck Ruxton, on September 14. Lancaster police found that Ruxton's wife, 34-year-old Isabella Van Ess, had also vanished.

When the police questioned Ruxton's neighbors, and searched the doctor's house, they found traces of blood and human fat in the drains. They compared the remains of the second body with known details of the housemaid, and found that the killer had made a huge effort to eliminate any special distinguishing features. Isabella Ruxton's corpse was also stripped of its identity. She had had a prominent nose and teeth, both of which had been removed. Every body part that might have provided further evidence had been cut away: the eyes, nose, ears, lips,

BACKGROUND Buck Ruxton with his wife and one of their children.

BELOW LEFT TO RIGHT A photograph of Mrs Ruxton used to identify the skull.

A picture of Mrs Ruxton's skull, taken to match the position on the photograph.

The skull picture superimposed on the photograph of Mrs Ruxton.

and fingertips had been removed, which pointed to the killer having expert medical knowledge. Isabella's remains were finally positively identified by superimposing a photograph of her over the skull of the victim. The match was conclusive. Dr. Ruxton was tried and convicted for the murder of the two women. He was executed in 1936.

PURE POISON

Was it an accident? Suicide? Or cold-blooded murder? Poison creates many questions and problems for people investigating suspicious deaths. The wide range of concoctions can mislead medical examiners when they produce physical symptoms that resemble those of common but fatal diseases. The chemicals involved, however, are usually not widely available for purchase, so users tend to be professionals such as doctors or pharmacists. Today, poisoning accounts for only around one in every hundred murders in countries where highly skilled medical and forensic services exist, such as the United States, Canada and in Europe.

Who administered the fatal dose?

Poisons can be responsible in cases other than murder where forensic evidence is needed to establish cause of death. Accidental poisoning, for example, usually results from mistakes being made with medical prescriptions. Such accidents can also occur when household chemicals, such as weed-killers or strong cleaning preparations, are stored in unlabeled bottles or simply left where young children can reach them.

Suicide poisoning usually involves substances such as painkillers or sleeping tablets that are commonly available in restricted doses but, if taken in excess, can be fatal. For example, relatively large doses of chloral hydrate, which is used medicinally as a sedative and hypnotic, will cause a coma followed

BELOW Domestic medicines, sometimes used by suicides.

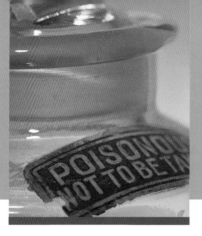

by death in a matter of hours from heart and respiratory failure. Strong or corrosive household or garden chemicals can also kill a person. They may be used by a victim who, intending to cause his or her own death, has no need to hide this fact.

Murderers' poisons

The criminal's most important requirement: that the poison should be lethal but at the same time produce symptoms that suggest another, less suspicious, cause of death. At one time many poisons were extracted from plants and vegetables, so people who knew what they were looking for had little trouble obtaining them.

Aconitine, which is extracted from the flowers and roots of a plant called monkshood, was once the most lethal poison known. It was used to treat rheumatism by being applied to areas of skin, where it produced a warming and painkilling action. Once in the body, an extremely small dose of aconitine can be lethal, paralyzing all the body's organs in succession until the victim dies of heart failure or suffocation.

Atropine can be extracted from plants such as deadly nightshade. It produces headaches, giddiness, hallucinations and finally a coma which ends in death from heart or respiratory failure. Where atropine has been ingested, the subject's pupils dilate and heavy doses can make the eyes appear almost completely black.

ABOVE Herod the Great (74–4 BC) being reproached by his wife for the murder of her father and brother. In the foreground is Salome with a chalice (goblet) of poison for the king, sent by his wife.

TOP "Poisonous" warning on a stoppered chemical bottle.

Fueled by carbon monoxide

One of the most common accidental or suicide poisons is carbon monoxide, a gas which is generated by automobile exhausts and sometimes by faulty gas appliances. Suicides often pipe the exhaust into a car through a length of vacuum-cleaner or garden hose, or run an automobile engine in a closed garage. When the carbon monoxide is inhaled it combines in place of oxygen with the hemoglobin in the red blood cells. Gradually the victim's blood becomes saturated with carboxy-hemoglobin instead of the normal oxy-hemoglobin. He or she suffocates internally from this lack of oxygen. In such cases, the outward appearance of the victim usually gives the forensic examiner enough initial evidence about the cause of death, since the presence of carboxy-hemoglobin in the blood turns the skin and the internal organs a bright cherry red.

Suicide attempt, using carbon monoxide from car exhaust.

ABOVE Baby food poisoned with arsenic by blackmailer Rodney Witchelo in England in the 1980s.

Strychnine is a highly toxic vegetable alkaloid obtained chiefly from the *Strychnos nux-vomica* shrub found in the Indian subcontinent, where it was used in very small doses to build up immunity to bites from poisonous snakes. A dose of just one fiftieth of a gram of this intensely bitter-tasting extract can be fatal. It produces violent muscular contractions: the victim is rendered speechless by paralysis of the jaw, the lips are drawn back into a bizarre-looking grin, and eventually death results from paralysis of the respiratory system. At one time, such deaths were usually attributed to tetanus or to severe epileptic fits. But once a reliable test for the presence of strychnine was developed, criminals were forced to turn to more subtle methods.

Yet another powerful poison, thallium, offers would-be murderers a number of advantages. Several different compounds containing the metal dissolve invisibly and tastelessly in water. Once in the body, thallium substitutes itself for potassium in different body systems that nourish cells and nerve fibers. As a result, the patient becomes weaker and eventually dies from the cumulative internal damage. The outward symptoms, however, can be confused with those of influenza except that thallium poisoning causes the victim's hair to fall out as the toxin begins its work.

ABOVE Hair loss characteristic of thallium poisoning. Jethro Batt was a victim of English poisoner Graham Young.

By contrast, the chemical element antimony, administered in repeated small doses, produces symptoms resembling those of several stomach diseases. Sickness, pains in the stomach, loss of appetite, and diarrhea lead to extreme depression, painful cramps and convulsions, and finally heart failure.

Arsenic, much loved by criminals and crime-writers alike, has a taste that can be disguised by food, and symptoms produced by repeated small doses can look like those induced by severe food poisoning or even cholera and dysentery. Arsenic is an irritant poison and victims usually suffer from burning in the throat, nausea, sickness, stomach pains and cramps. By the time the patient dies, traces of arsenic are present in all the body tissues.

ABOVE A scanning electron microscope, used to examine the pellet that held ricin–the poison responsible for the death of Georgi Markov in 1978 (see pages 126–7).

Cyanide works in the same way as carbon monoxide–by starving the blood of life-giving oxygen–but it works much more quickly, causing death within minutes. One characteristic sign of cyanide poisoning is a bitter almond smell which tends to linger in the mouth of victims and can be detected in the stomach contents.

Some of the deadliest natural poisons are found in fungi. Their efficacy as poison is partly due to their subtlety: by the time any symptoms are recognizable, the poison is already well established. The genus *Amanita* (which includes *Amanita phalloides* or the

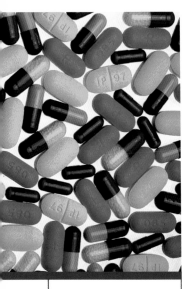

ABOVE An assortment of medical pills, tablets, and capsules.

BELOW Fields of opium growing in Afghanistan, one of the prime producers of this drug.

"death cap," the most dangerous fungus known) can cause intense suffering and often death even if taken in only the smallest quantities. The toxin works by destroying the body's cell nuclei. A side-effect is a speeding-up of the heartbeat, which in turn accelerates the spread of the poison through the system.

Ricin, derived from the seed of the castor-oil plant, is one of the more exotic poisons. It causes the victim's red blood cells to clump together and then attacks the other body cells, causing a high temperature followed by vomiting and eventually death from heart failure. Because it is exceptionally deadly, there have been rumors ricin could be a potential biological weapon, used for military purposes. However, its only recorded use as a poison was in the murder of Bulgarian dissident Georgi Markov.

Highs and hallucinations

Overdosing on narcotics and hallucinogenic drugs causes cumulative poisoning of the body system. These can result from individual reactions to individual drugs and from contamination of the drug being used in an individual case.

Not all narcotic drugs are derived from opium, and a number of synthetic drugs that have similar effects on the body are commonly described as opiates. These include methadone, which has been used in rehabilitation programs in order to wean addicts from using heroin and other drugs. Another opiate, propoxyphene, was originally marketed as a painkiller in the late 1950s and has since been implicated in cases of addiction and overdoses.

Other drugs that are classified as depressants also work to depress the action of the central nervous system. These include alcohol, the most widely used drug of all in the Western world, and also a wide variety of tranquilizers, barbiturates and the volatile chemicals contained in adhesive solvents, lighter fuels and hairsprays, which can be inhaled to produce the depressant effect. In general, these substances produce a feeling of relaxation, euphoria, exhilaration and ultimately drowsiness and sleep. In all cases, large doses can be harmful or even fatal.

The poison detectives

Faced with a victim of poisoning, forensic scientists have a daunting array of possible agents to search for at autopsy. The procedure often starts with samples of the victim's blood, urine or specific tissues being dissolved in an acidified or alkaline solution. Acidified water is used when looking for evidence of acidic drugs such as ASA or barbiturates, which can be extracted from the solution using organic solvents such as chloroform.

A screening test can check quite rapidly for a wide range of drugs or poisons. Complicated mixtures can be broken down into their constituent parts using a technique called gas chromatography. More recently, forensic laboratories have been turning to immuno-assay techniques to test samples for very small amounts of drugs or poisons. This involves the development of antibodies that react with the substances investigators are looking at. First, the drug in question is combined with a protein and the compound injected into the bloodstream of an animal. This stimulates the animal to produce antibodies, which are extracted from a blood sample, then added to the test sample. If the drug in question is present in the test sample, the antibodies from the animal's blood will be seen to react with it.

Confirmation tests usually involve a combination of gas chromatography and mass spectrometry. As each different component from the sample mixture emerges from the chromatography column, it enters into a mass spectrometer. There, it is bombarded by a stream of high-energy electrons. They cause the component to break up, producing a different but characteristic spectrum for each individual substance present.

ABOVE Forensic narcotic tests: a selection of vials used by police officers at the scene of a crime to test for illegal narcotics. Each vial is marked with the narcotic it can identify (from left; opiates and amphetamines; cannabis; LSD; cocaine).

BELOW Indian Hemp (*Cannabis sativa*), also known as pot, marijuana, or hashish.

CAROLINE GRILLS

Aunt Thally's poisoned tea

The death of an 87-year-old Australian woman named Christina Mickelson in Sydney, Australia, in the 1940s seemed natural enough. When family friend Angeline Thomas died not long afterward, this too seemed reasonable because she was also in her eighties. But when a much younger relative, 60-year-old John Lundberg, died the very next year. that looked more suspicious. Lundberg's hair had fallen out before he died, which made it all the more alarming when another family member, Mary Ann Mickelson, fell ill with similar symptoms before she too finally died.

One factor common to all four deaths was the presence of 63-year-old Caroline Grills. Grills, who had married Mrs. Mickelson's stepson nearly 40 years earlier, had nursed Christina Mickelson through her final illness. When Angeline Thomas fell ill, Grills had helped to care for her, too, preparing endless cups of tea–supposedly to lift the invalid's spirits. She had also tended John Lundberg and Mary Ann Mickelson. One after another, her patients all became sicker until eventually they died.

By 1948, the mystery sickness was threatening the lives of John Lundberg's widow and daughter, who both grew steadily sicker, despite Caroline Grills' attentive care. Both women were losing their hair and complained they were severely tired. A suspicious relative alerted the local police, who removed one of the cups of tea Grills had made for the suffering women and analyzed it.

OPPOSITE A picture of Caroline Grills, who used thallium to poison her victims.

The victims' hair had fallen out during their illnesses, so investigators looked for the presence of the poison thallium. Laboratory technicians used the Reinsch test, which involves adding the suspect material to a solution of hydrochloric acid. Next, they dipped a copper strip into the resulting mixture to see if any metallic deposit would form on it, showing the presence of a heavy metal, such as arsenic, antimony, or thallium. When contamination shows up, further analysis can confirm exactly which metal is present.

Investigators found out that thallium had been added to the tea. Fortunately, they discovered this in time to save the lives of Mrs. Lundberg and her daughter, although Mrs. Lundberg lost her eyesight because she had absorbed so much poison into her system.

Caroline Grills was tried and found guilty of the attempted murder of Mrs. Lundberg and sentenced to life imprisonment. She was popular among the other inmates who came to nickname her "Aunt Thally."

GEORGI MARKOV

and the poisonous pellet

Georgi Markov was a Bulgarian dissident working for the BBC World Service in London, broadcasting to his former homeland. On the afternoon of September 7, 1978, he was waiting for a bus on Waterloo Bridge when he felt a sharp stabbing pain in his right thigh. He turned to see a man carrying a folded-up umbrella; the man mumbled an apology in a thick accent and hurried off to hail a cab.

TOP Bulgarian dissident Georgi Markov was the second expatriate to be attacked by agents of the Government of Bulgaria.

ABOVE Photomicrograph of the fatal pellet that was recovered from Markov's body.

Once home, Markov inspected the wound–a small red puncture mark at the back of his leg. By the following morning, he was vomiting and running a high fever. After he was taken to hospital, the wound, now inflamed, was X-rayed, but nothing suspicious showed up on the films. Meanwhile, Markov's temperature and blood-pressure were dropping and his pulse racing. His white-cell count soared to three times the normal level and doctors suspected blood poisoning. He was treated with antibiotics but became delirious and experienced violent fits. Four days after the mysterious wound was inflicted, Georgi Markov died.

An autopsy was carried out and the section of tissue that contained the puncture wound was sent to the Porton Down chemical warfare research laboratories. Buried beneath the skin, experts found a spherical pellet approximately the size of a pinhead with two tiny holes drilled in it. However, no trace could be found of any poison that might have caused Markov's illness and death.

The pellet was sent to the Metropolitan Police forensic laboratory where it was examined under a scanning electron microscope. It proved to be made of an alloy of platinum and iridium with holes just large enough to hold a minute trace of poison, but their contents had dissipated. Examiners guessed that the tiny pellet had been fired by some form of gas-operated gun hidden in the stranger's furled umbrella in a bid to assassinate Markov. Considering the minute size of the dose and its catastrophic effects, it seemed likely that the pellet was charged with ricin (see page 32). Ricin is a potential chemical warfare agent 500 times more lethal than the poison cyanide.

The Bulgarians denied any responsibility for the murder. However, another expatriate Bulgarian named Vladimir Kostov had suffered a similar attack in Paris a year earlier, but had recovered because the pellet had been fired into his back, far away from the main blood vessels. When a surgeon examined Kostov, an identical pellet was found buried beneath his skin. Following a change of regime in Bulgaria in 1991, the new government admitted that assassination attempts had been made on a number of former citizens living in the West, including Markov and Kostov.

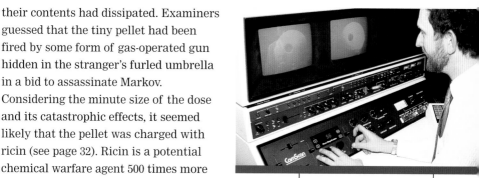

ABOVE Scanning electron microscope used to examine the fatal pellet.

BELOW The specialized pellet gun concealed in the furled umbrella and used to murder Markov.

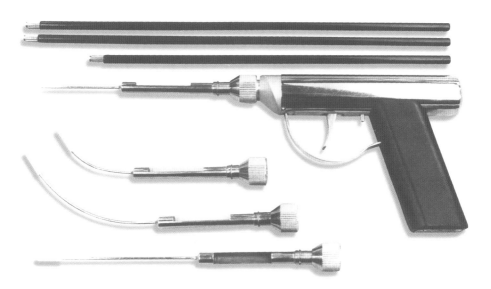

THE CUT OF A KNIFE; THE BLOW OF A HAMMER

Knives and blunt instruments, frequently messy, are the cruder weapons that criminals employ. Often, they resort to these objects for an unplanned attack or because more sophisticated weapons, such as firearms, are not available. They may wield a stiletto, a switchblade, or kitchen knife, or reach for the nearest heavy object that can cause sufficient damage, be it a wrench, a hammer, a lamp, or a chunk of wood.

When tackling such a case, forensic scientists try to prove that a particular weapon was the one used in a given murder. Or, if the murder weapon is missing, they aim to describe it, based on the victim's injuries, so investigators know what to look for while they track down more evidence.

A battered testimony

When someone is battered to death with a blunt instrument, the blows are usually delivered to the head, and a single blow is rarely enough to kill the

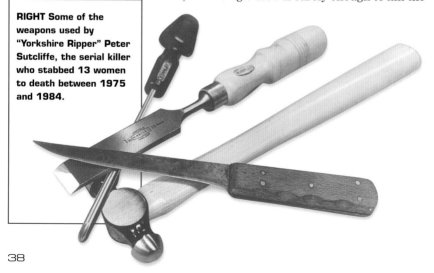

RIGHT Some of the weapons used by "Yorkshire Ripper" Peter Sutcliffe, the serial killer who stabbed 13 women to death between 1975 and 1984.

victim. Examination of the head typically reveals a series of blows, each of which can cause ragged lacerations where scraps of tissue and blood vessels are pressed into the surface of the underlying bones. The head may show depression fractures where the bones of the skull were driven into the brain tissues, causing death by compression of the brain. In such cases, the shape of the fractured area may provide clues about the shape of the weapon that the attacker used.

TOP Mummified head of *Lindow Man*, dated between 20 and 130 ad, who met a violent end, being struck on the head and garroted, a method of strangling.

BELOW Pauline Parker (pictured below), along with Juliet Hume, battered Parker's mother to death in New Zealand, 1954. Forensic evidence in Parker's diary exposed the lie that the victim had slipped and fallen to her death.

Sometimes the fatal injuries are only part of the evidence found on the victim's body. If the attack was prolonged, or a physical struggle preceded the murder, patterns of bruising may yield major clues about what happened. Bruises, caused by the breaking of small blood vessels beneath the skin, can give forensic experts some idea about the series of events during the attack, and where and how the fatal blow was struck. Examination can also reveal whether the blood vessels ruptured before or after death. For example, in cases where bruising occurred before death, blood samples will usually show a higher-than-normal white cell count, which shows the body's attempt to respond to an injury.

A wound at close range

Murders with knives tend to be the most common type of killing in countries where gun-control laws are strictly enforced. Even in the United States, knife murders rank

ABOVE Peter Sutcliffe, the "Yorkshire Ripper", a former mortuary worker.

second to those involving guns. Knife wounds are almost always inflicted during close-range attacks. In the case of incised wounds, where the attacker makes a series of slashing moves, a victim's arms and hands often show cuts that resulted from attempts to ward off the blows in self-defense. Struggles of this kind usually leave the attacker spattered or even drenched in the victim's blood. Such bloodstains, if found, offer positive proof that the attacker was present during the assault.

Signs of suicide

Forensic Fact

Although people rarely commit suicide with a knife, those who do usually target one of three sites on the body: they attempt to cut the throat, or to stab themselves in the chest or stomach. In cases where a person stabs him- or herself through the heart or stomach, there are usually just one or two intentional stabs. Most victims remove the clothing over the target area and they locate the wound within easy reach so they can deliver it with enough force.

When a person commits suicide by cutting the throat, the evidence often shows one or two shallower gashes. These are caused by "trial attempts" the person makes while building up enough determination to deliver the final, lethal cut.

Forensic experts recognize another basic type of knife wound. Stab wounds are inflicted when a knife blade is pushed into the body, damaging the body's vital organs and producing internal bleeding. In these cases there may be relatively little external bleeding and, if the knife is removed, the stab wound can shrink, making it appear less obvious than an incised wound. In order to cause death, stab wounds require a blade long enough to penetrate the chest or abdomen.

Careful inspection of a stab wound can reveal useful details about the type of weapon that was used. A skilled anthropologist can often tell whether the wound resulted from a double-edged blade or a blade with only one sharp edge. Or perhaps the victim was stabbed with another object, such as a chisel, a screwdriver or a pair of scissors. To learn more about the shape and form of the weapon, experts may use an elaborate technique to produce a cast of the wound. To do this, they dissect layer by layer the part of the victim's body that contains the wound in order to build up a three-dimensional representation. In at least one case, the victim's chest, and the fatal wound, were preserved in a chemical called formalin after the autopsy. After the murder weapon was found and presented as evidence, prosecutors were able to demonstrate in court that the shape of the weapon matched that of the wound.

BELOW In the case of one murdered woman, a pathologist found a knife blade tip in a neck wound. It fitted the broken blade of a penknife found in the pants pocket of her husband, the accused.

JEFFREY MACDONALD

and the ice pick

Jeffrey MacDonald was a captain in the U.S. Army, living with his wife Colette and two young daughters at Fort Bragg in North Carolina. Military police responding to an emergency telephone call from the home around 3:30 a.m. on February 17, 1970 found his pregnant wife and both daughters dead from numerous stab wounds. MacDonald was alive and claimed he had been stabbed and knocked unconscious by three men and a woman, whom he described as

"hippies". He told police he had resisted their frenzied blows by wrapping his blue pajama jacket around his hands, and explained how, after the attackers fled, he had first tried to resuscitate his daughters, then placed the jacket over his dead wife's body.

MacDonald gave detailed descriptions of all four attackers, but police found no evidence of their presence. Officers distrusted MacDonald's story because the room was dark at the time of the attack, and MacDonald had very poor eyesight. He needed glasses to read and to drive, so without them, his vision would have been blurred. When a forensic team searched the scene, they found blue fibers from his pajama jacket beneath his wife's body, in the children's bedrooms and under the fingernail of one victim. But no blue fibers were found in the living room where MacDonald claimed he had fought for his life and the room showed very little disorder. Bloodstains in the different rooms were all identified, and MacDonald's blood was found in the kitchen, in the bathroom and on a pair of eyeglasses. No traces were found where he said he had been stabbed, or on the telephone he had used to call the police.

TOP U.S. Army Captain Jeffrey MacDonald.

ABOVE A military policeman stands guard as a crime lab technician works inside the MacDonald home.

Nevertheless, by the time MacDonald's trial was due, many pieces of evidence had been lost and the charges were dropped. When he subsequently appeared on a television chat show, his callous attitude and flippant remarks made about the deaths revived suspicions that he had committed the crimes. Police sent his pajama jacket to the FBI laboratory in Washington, D. C. for analysis. Investigators concluded that all 48 holes (which MacDonald said were made by the attackers' ice pick) were smooth and round, which indicated that someone had held the jacket still when the holes were made.

There was also a large stain of Colette MacDonald's blood on both sides of a tear that MacDonald said was made during the attack. This suggested that the stain had been produced before the jacket was torn, although MacDonald claimed to have laid the jacket across his wife's body after the attack ended.

In 1979, MacDonald was brought to trial. Forensic examiners presented a simulated attack in the courtroom with an ice pick and a pajama jacket. They showed that the pattern of cuts made in MacDonald's pajama jacket was not consistent with the pattern that would have resulted if the events unfolded as MacDonald originally claimed. As a result, MacDonald was found guilty and ordered to serve three consecutive life sentences.

ABOVE MacDonald pictured on the day before he was accused of killing his pregnant wife and his children.

BELOW The bedroom where the two young daughters died.

43

CHAPTER 5

STARVED OF AIR: STRANGULATION AND SUFFOCATION

BELOW Michael Hutchence, leader of the musical group **INXS**, who allegedly committed suicide by hanging in 1997.

A cord, a rope, a length of wire or the murderer's own hands; a pillow or plastic bag over the face, or a weight pressed on the victim's chest. These are the weapons of the strangler–methods that literally take a person's breath away through strangulation or suffocation. By examining the scene and the body, forensic scientists try to figure out how the victim died, sometimes defeating the criminal's best efforts to cover his or her tracks or to hide the fact that a crime was even committed.

Accidental suffocation

Rather than being purposely killed, a victim can be starved of air unintentionally because of where he or she happens to be. Victims can also be accidentally suffocated by what is described as crush asphyxia. This can occur when a victim is trapped in a crowd or by a fall in a mine or quarry, or by falling concrete in an earthquake. Breathing becomes impossible as the weight of other people or of the debris squeezes the chest. In cases of crush asphyxia, examiners often observe signs of hemorrhaging from the head and chest and around the eyeballs, which are often full of excess fluid.

Murderous hands

The pressure of unwanted hands around the throat that cuts off of the blood supply to the brain, unconsciousness, and death–this is the dreadful ending suffered by the strangler's target. To a

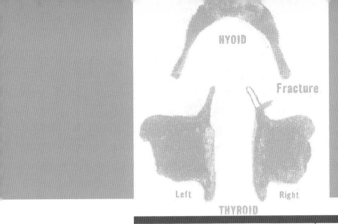

HYOID

Fracture

Left   Right

THYROID

forensic scientist, the body of a victim of manual strangulation shows clear signs of what has happened. In order to cut off both respiration and blood circulation, the attacker has to apply enough force to cause bruising of the victim's neck and throat. The bruises, which result from the pressure of the thumbs and fingertips, are usually rather circular in shape and about a $1/2$ inch in diameter. Fingernails tearing into the victim's skin may produce curved marks.

Strangulation produces still other physical signs in the victim. A tongue trapped between the teeth may show bite marks and bruising of the tissues. More bruising may occur in the surrounding area,

ABOVE Damage to the larynx by a fracture to the hyoid shows that the victim has been strangled.

BELOW The sensitive skin around the neck can reveal bruises from the strangler's fingers or abrasion from a strangling cord.

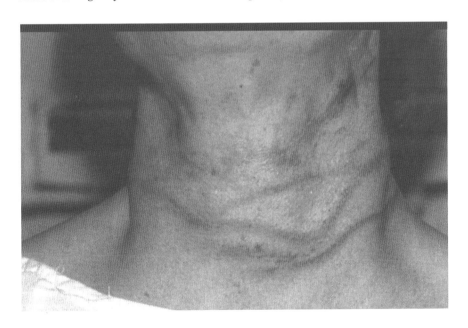

ABOVE Re-enactment of a murder by hanging at Blackfriars Bridge, London.

including the lining of the larynx, the voice box and the floor of the mouth. As with any death from strangulation, the hyoid bone, a curved bone at the base of the tongue, will probably have been broken. And if the attacker used a great deal of force, the cartilage of the windpipe and larynx may also be fractured. Another mark of strangulation is the presence of pinpoint hemorrhages around the eyes.

Hanging—a jump or a push?

The scene of a hanging usually divulges all too clearly what has happened. Nonetheless, forensic examiners still face two main questions: First, did the victim die from hanging, or was he or she already dead before the body was hanged? And second, did the victim die as a result of the hanging, or was it murder or suicide?

Whether the hanging was self-inflicted or the work of a killer, the effects of asphyxia usually can be seen, especially on the victim's face. When the oxygen supply to the blood fails, the deoxygenated blood turns a characteristic blue color, which shows on the lips and tongue. Often, the tongue protrudes between the lips, the pupils of the eyes are dilated, and the face is literally deathly pale because the rope cuts off the blood supply to the head. Since these effects can also be caused by straightforward strangulation, forensic examiners closely scrutinize the victim's neck to detect any bruising or other injuries that would not have been caused by a noose. They search the scene of the hanging to uncover inconsistencies if they suspect someone has deliberately tried to confuse the picture. For example, a genuine suicide, found hanging clear of the ground, would have stood on a ladder or a chair while putting on the noose, so this kind of object would be found at the scene.

The tools of strangulation

Is there a horizontal groove low down on the neck? This would suggest that the victim was strangled by

Forensic Fact

Examining the clues

Death by asphyxiation results when air is prevented from reaching the lungs. A victim of strangling often dies because the supply of blood and oxygen to the brain is cut off (1 and 2).

Excess pressure on the vagus nerve during strangulation can cause it to send a signal to the brain ordering the heart to stop beating (3).

Separation of the vertebrae (bones in the spinal column) can rupture blood vessels and tear the spinal cord, causing instant death (4).

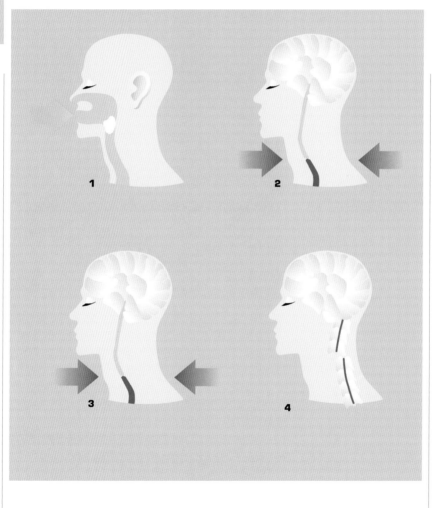

"Burking"

Forensic Fact

The notorious 19th-century "bodysnatchers" Burke and Hare made a living by murdering victims to sell their bodies to the anatomy departments of teaching hospitals in Edinburgh, Scotland. Because these bodies had to be in good condition, with no external injuries, these murderers perfected a method of killing that criminals and police later called "Burking." Kneeling on the victim's chest, Burke and Hare used their hands to close off the nose and mouth.

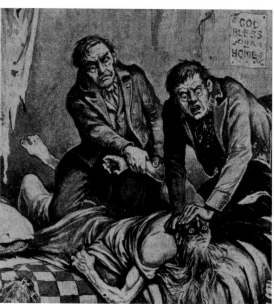

Burke and Hare suffocating one of their victims, to sell the corpse to teaching hospitals where medical students would dissect them as part of their training.

a ligature, such as rope or cord, rather than hanged, because a hanged body falls into the ligature under gravity. By examining the appearance of the marks, forensic scientists can deduce what type of ligature was used. A deep and narrow mark indicates some form of wire, cord or cable, while a broader, shallower scar is more likely to have been caused by a tie, a belt, pantyhose or a scarf, for example.

If the ligature is found at the scene, it can provide vital evidence in solving the puzzle. The material used may have a link with the victim or, more importantly, with the attacker. Even the way in which the ligature is used can provide clues. When the infamous Boston Strangler killed 13 people in the early 1960s, he tied his ligature in a characteristic knot, which identified each of the deaths as his handiwork.

The use of a ligature requires less pressure on the victim than is needed with manual strangulation. As a result, investigators find less obvious bruising around the neck and, sometimes, less muscular damage. The cartilage of the larynx and windpipe also may be intact, although there may be damage to the thyroid cartilage and neck muscles. Blood in the brain tissues may reveal other hemorrhages.

Some victims found dead with a ligature around the neck are suicides. In such cases, the victim usually deliberately ties the ligature with a double knot in order to maintain the pressure even as he or she loses consciousness. However in suicide cases, the hyoid bone is usually found to be intact, another clue that may help investigators unravel the truth.

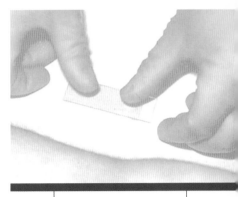

ABOVE A pathologist applies transparent adhesive tape to a ligature mark to lift any fibers onto paper for microscopic examination.

BELOW LEFT Murder equipment used by British serial killer Denis Nilson to torture and kill his victims.

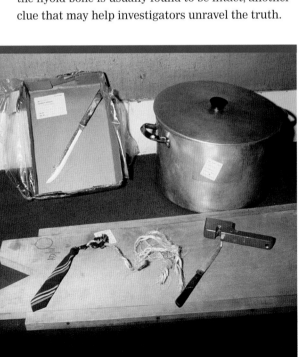

A TRUNK FULL OF CLUES

In the summer of 1889, people living in the small riverside community of Millery near Lyon in southern France were disturbed by a terrible smell. A council workman was sent to investigate, and he found a rotting corpse, tied up in a canvas sack, among bushes by the riverbank. The remains were taken to the Lyon city morgue, a barge on the River Rhône. There the local forensic pathologist, Dr. Paul Bernard, began his examination.

ABOVE This engraving shows a reconstruction of the Gouffé murder.

Though the identity of the body was a mystery, Dr. Bernard found injuries to the neck that indicated the victim had died from strangulation, possibly with a ligature. Evidence from the skull led him to guess that the victim's age had been about 35.

The investigation progressed more quickly after investigators turned up a trunk that smelled as strongly as the body and had almost certainly been used to transport it. Labels in the trunk showed that it had been sent from Paris to Lyon just over two weeks before the corpse was discovered. Checks of the missing persons files in Paris revealed that a notorious womanizer called Toussaint-Augsent Gouffé had been reported missing on the same day the trunk had been dispatched to Lyon.

But police soon questioned their theory that the corpse was that of the missing Gouffé when the man's brother-in-law reported that Gouffé had chestnut-colored hair: the hair and beard of the corpse were both jet black. When Dr. Bernard soaked a hair sample in distilled water, however, the black dissolved to reveal a bright chestnut color.

The corpse was then delivered to Dr. Alexandre Lacassagne, France's foremost criminal pathologist and a pioneer of scientific detection. Dr. Lacassagne, professor of forensic medicine at the University of Lyon, was convinced that death had been caused by manual strangulation. Examination of the bones also showed a defect in the right knee, which would have produced a definite limp. After studying the victim's teeth, Lacassagne raised Dr. Bernard's estimate of the victim's age to about 50. Since Gouffé had been 49 and had walked with a noticeable limp, the identity of the victim seemed certain, especially when samples of hair from the corpse were matched with hairs from Gouffé's own hairbrush.

A huge publicity campaign, aided by a replica of the trunk used to carry Gouffé's remains to Lyon, produced a pair of suspects: Michel Eyraud and his mistress Gabrielle Bompard, who had been seen buying a similar trunk in Paris. Later, police learned that the pair had lured Gouffé to Bompard's apartment, where they intended to kill him before raiding his offices. They tried to hang him by winding Bompard's dressing-gown cord around his neck and then passing it over an overhead pulley, but the knot failed to hold.

Eyraud then resorted to strangling Gouffé with his bare hands, after which the couple ransacked his office but failed to find most of his money. After sending the trunk with Gouffé's remains to Lyon, the pair fled to North America. When Eyraud suggested repeating the crime with a new male victim, they parted company, and Bompard returned to France. Eyraud was caught almost two years later in Cuba, and finally extradited to France where both of them were tried for murder. Bompard was sentenced to 20 years in prison, and Eyraud was executed by guillotine.

ABOVE Engraving showing the arrest of Michel Eyraud in Havana, Cuba.

BELOW A replica of the trunk used to transport the remains of Gouffé's body, which was first identified by its smell.

FIRE AND WATER: DEATH BY BURNING AND DROWNING

Deaths by drowning or burning usually result from tragic accidents. However, forensic experts still must check carefully to confirm that the circumstances are what they appear to be and have not been used to cover up a more sinister death.

ABOVE Paramedics and doctors tend to injured victim at fire scene.

Whenever any dead body is found in the water, forensic scientists must decide whether the victim died of drowning or hypothermia as a result of being in the water, or whether he or she was already dead before entering the water. Similar questions arise in cases of burning: Was the body deliberately burned in order to disguise some other cause of death? The corpse is checked thoroughly to determine which injuries were caused by burning, whether or not those injuries were inflicted before or after death, and which factors actually caused the death.

Evidence of drowning

A person drowns when water enters the lungs. This produces a thin, frothy mixture of water, air and mucus that appears at the mouth and nostrils. The weight of water in the lungs causes the body to swell and increase in weight so that a drowning victim tends to float lower in the water than a live person would.

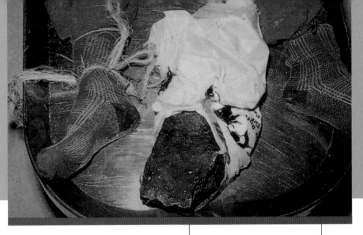

The autopsy provides more detailed evidence. After death by drowning, the lungs appear waterlogged and swollen. They are soft to the touch, so that pressure on the surface of the lungs leaves a mark that takes longer to fade. The frothy mixture of water, air and mucus that appears in the nose and mouth will also show up in the victim's windpipe and lungs, and in many cases, water is found in the throat and stomach. The stomach may also contain organisms from the water in which the body was found. In addition, most genuine drowning victims have hemorrhages in the middle ear that would not occur if, for example, they died from heart failure or upon falling into the water.

In some apparent drowning cases, the victim does not actually die from drowning but from the shock of suddenly being plunged into cold water. This condition is called "reflex cardiac arrest." In these cases, investigators will not find the normal signs of drowning on the body.

The flow of time

Bodies undergo a different process of decay in water than they do when they are buried or left exposed on land. First of all, in water the cooling process after death occurs twice as quickly. When a victim dies because of hypothermia rather than by drowning, the core temperature of the body may already be significantly lower than normal when the process of post-mortem cooling begins to set in.

A corpse immersed in water also has less obvious post-mortem discoloration. Instead, the skin appears

ABOVE London's King's Cross Tube disaster, in 1987, where smoke and fire poured through a crowded subway station.

BELOW A case of severe burns caused by the hot fat from a frying pan.

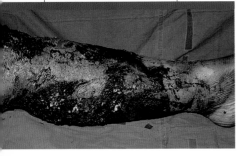

unnaturally white, with a "goose-flesh" effect from when the body's hair follicles became erect, a reflex intended to retain body heat as long as possible. *Rigor mortis* can take up to four days to develop and will take longer to disappear because the water temperature slows down the chemical processes that trigger these post-mortem changes.

After a week or more in the water, chemical changes within the body cause the abdomen to fill with gas. The body becomes more buoyant so that it floats on the surface of the water. As a result, many drowning victims who are not retrieved earlier tend to be found at this stage.

Six degrees of burning

As with cases of drowning, investigators look for specific clues when examining the bodies of burn victims. Burn injuries are classified both in terms of the percentage of the body area that is affected and in terms of their severity. The six degrees of burn injuries were first classified by French surgeon Baron Guillaume Dupuytren nearly two centuries ago. First-degree burns cause the skin to become inflamed and swollen and scales of the skin surface are shed. Second-degree burns show blistering, while third- and fourth-degree burns show partial or entire destruction of the victim's skin, and fifth-degree burns destroy the muscles. Sixth-degree burns, the most severe, also show bone destruction.

Many victims found in burned-out structures die from smoke suffocation or carbon monoxide poisoning rather than the burns themselves. Blood tests can show the presence of carbon monoxide at a level high enough to cause death, while the presence of any carbon monoxide or soot within the victim's body confirms he or she was still alive when the fire started. If these signs are not found, then the victim must have been dead before the blaze took hold.

Examination of the victim's burns can help investigators chart the sequence of events. In general, burns suffered while the victim was still alive have a higher proportion of white cells in the blood count, because the body mobilized its natural defenses at the time in an effort to contain the damage. Fluid from the blisters at the site of the burns can also be tested for proteins. Their presence shows that the victim was alive when the blisters formed.

ABOVE A victim of Wayne Williams (see pages 96-97) lies face down in a boat after being pulled from the Chattahoochee river.

Locating the watery grave

Where did the drowning take place? Investigators may find out by probing body organs for the presence of tiny organisms called diatoms—microscopic algae-like creatures. These are present in all water sources that contain normal biosystems. A drowning victim inhales these organisms along with the water that causes the drowning, and they are absorbed into the internal organs. During the autopsy, sections of the internal organs are dissolved in strong acids, a process that will reveal the silica shells of the diatoms if they are present.

The presence of diatoms gives two useful clues. First, it indicates that the victim was almost certainly alive when he or she entered the water. Second, there are many different species of these organisms. By identifying the species or combination of species of diatoms found in the victim's body, investigators may figure out the approximate area where the original drowning took place.

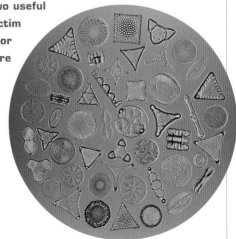

Diatoms, microscopic algae-like creatures found in the lungs, stomach, bloodstream and bone marrow of drowning victims.

ROBERT
MAXWELL
afloat

In the fall of 1991, British publisher and newspaper tycoon Robert Maxwell was cruising in his luxury yacht, the *Lady Ghislaine*. One morning the crew was shocked to find he was no longer on board. He had last been seen on deck the evening before. A search was made and his dead body was eventually found in the sea off the Canary Islands in the northeast Atlantic Ocean. The enquiry into Maxwell's death came under the jurisdiction of the Spanish authorities, because the Canary Islands group is Spanish territory.

At the time, the press speculated that Maxwell's death might be connected to his known links with Israel and his rumored involvement with Mossad, the Israeli intelligence service. Some people suggested that these connections may have made him the target of a sophisticated professional assassination. Had that been true, Maxwell would almost certainly have been dead before he entered the water. Otherwise, the alarm might have been raised and he could have been rescued.

Spanish experts carried out an autopsy and found that diatoms were present in Maxwell's blood and body tissues, showing clearly that he had died after he entered the water. There was no evidence of other injuries to suggest that a murder attempt had taken place. But, curiously, Maxwell's lungs were not full of water. This could have been due to a condition known as "dry drowning," where the shock of falling into the

BELOW Robert Maxwell shortly before his death in 1991.

ABOVE Maxwell's yacht, the *Lady Ghislaine*.

LEFT Maxwell on board the *Lady Ghislaine* from which he disappeared.

BELOW Maxwell's body was found floating 12 hours after his disappearance and became the subject of a detailed and lengthy investigation.

water causes a spasm of the larynx. This triggers a body reflex that resembles the physical reaction to a sudden and severe increase in blood pressure: the heart stops, causing death within seconds. The only question the enquiry could not answer was whether Maxwell had entered the water accidentally or deliberately. Rumors said that his business empire was shaky and that could have motivated him to attempt suicide.

THE SMOKING GUN

Each used bullet has its own tale to tell since mass-produced rifled weapons were developed in the late 18th century. Rifling sends a bullet flying more predictably to its target, but, for forensic scientists, the major benefit is that it gives an individual identity to every single gun. When bullets are fired through the barrel, the rifling grooves create marks on the bullet's surface in a pattern unique to that weapon. A similar pattern of marks appears on any bullet fired from that weapon, because the material used to make bullets is softer than the material of the gun barrels.

Other vital forensic clues have become available since the introduction of bullets that are encapsulated with the explosive charge in a single cased cartridge. As a charge explodes within the barrel, it expands in both directions, driving the bullet forward and the cartridge case backward with considerable force against the breech of the weapon. The cartridge case, which is ejected as the shot is fired, provides key information. It is imprinted with imperfections in the face of the breech and of parts of the gun mechanism, such as the firing pin. Although these patterns vary from weapon to weapon, they are virtually identical on any cartridge case used in a particular firearm.

Firearm "fingerprints"

Once investigators identify the kind of weapon that was used in a crime, they must still make a positive

ID of an individual weapon–and that ID must be very precise. Firearms hold clues that can help them prove their case. The internal surfaces of an individual gun barrel carry fine lines or striations on both the grooves and the lands. These are caused by surface defects on the cutting tool that was used to make the barrel, or by chips of steel scratched across the barrel's internal surfaces by the action of the cutter. The striations present in the barrel of each individual gun produce a characteristic set of marks on any bullet fired from that barrel. By firing a test bullet from a suspect weapon, then lining it up in a comparison microscope alongside a bullet from the crime scene, investigators can make a positive match of these individual markings with a greater degree of accuracy.

Classes of weapon

Forensic Fact

In mass-produced guns, particular makes and models of weapons are given the same standardized characteristics. These include the barrel's internal diameter or caliber, the number of grooves in its rifling, and the direction in which the grooves spiral from the breech to the muzzle. Investigators can therefore deduce the make and class of the weapon from examining any bullets found at the scene of a crime or in the body of a gunshot victim.

Bullets and spent cartridges can provide vital evidence.

Chapter 7

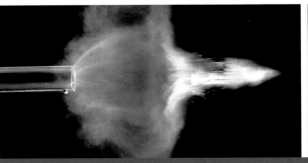
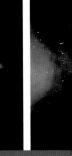

ABOVE, LEFT TO RIGHT
High speed photograph of a charge of pellets leaving the muzzle of a 12-bore shotgun, taken 2.8 milliseconds after detonation.

Four milliseconds after the cartridge detonates, a puff of smoke and gunpowder residues leave the barrel in the wake of the shot.

The plastic wad separating from the shot after 5.7 milliseconds.

After 7 milliseconds, particles of the wad that seals the front end of the cartridge falls away, and the charge of pellets begins to spread out.

BELOW Massed ranks of seized handguns in a court office.

The shotgun family

Different kinds of shotguns are also used in shooting crimes. Unlike other rifling weapons, shotguns do not fire a single bullet. Rather, the explosion of the charge in the cartridge of a shotgun releases a spray of small lead pellets which diverge as they fly through the air. Shotguns may be single- or double-barreled (with two barrels arranged either side by side or one on top of the other). Each of the two barrels usually needs to be reloaded once the cartridge has been fired.

Other types of shotgun, known as "pump-action" guns, carry several cartridges in an internal magazine, so the user can reload by pushing a slider backward and forward. Criminals sometimes use shotguns at short range. However, these guns are easier to hide when a foot or more is sawed off the length of the barrel. At almost point-blank range, where the shotgun is most dangerous to a human target, the spread of the pellets is slight.

Handguns and rifles

Handguns can be revolvers or pistols. Revolvers have a series of cartridges loaded into a cylindrical magazine that moves around at the discharge of each shot to bring the next round into the breech. These guns can be "single-action," where the user has to pull back the hammer to rotate the magazine and cock the firing mechanism, or "double-action," where this action occurs automatically by

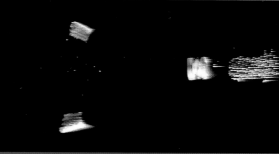

pressing hard on the trigger. Automatic pistols, on the other hand, usually have a series of rounds held in a vertical magazine inside the weapon's handle. To fire the weapon, the user only has to pull the trigger.

Rifles can be classified as target, sporting or military, and their actions vary much the same as handguns. Many rifles carry a series of rounds in an internal magazine, but most use a bolt action to reload. When the bolt is pulled back, the spent cartridge is ejected. When the bolt is pushed forward and turned, it pushes a new round into the breech and cocks the firing mechanism. Other rifles, particularly those designed for military use, eject the used round and load a new one automatically. So, again, all the user has to do is pull the trigger.

Telltale bullets and incriminating cartridges

For more than 150 years, the design of cartridges for both handguns and rifles has followed the same general pattern. A cylindrical cartridge case, usually made of brass, holds the main propellant charge used to fire the bullet. The front end of the cartridge is sealed by the bullet, and at the back a small cap contains a charge of primer. When the gun is fired, the firing pin strikes the cap and detonates the primer, which then sets off the main charge and fires the bullet straight down the barrel.

A ballistics expert can usually link the shape and design of the cartridge to a particular type and model of gun. Some cartridges have the primer cap in the center, while others have the primer arranged

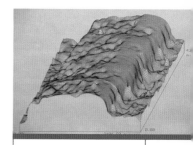

ABOVE Three-dimensional image of imperfections in a gun barrel.

BELOW Crime weapon being test-fired in a ballistics laboratory.

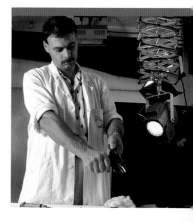

ABOVE Forensic examiner checking the clothing around a bullet hole for signs of the range at which the weapon was fired.

around the rim of the cartridge case. The bullets used in the cartridges also vary. All this information can help an expert to identify the ammunition used in a given incident.

Most pistols and rifles used for sport or target-shoot purposes use soft lead bullets. These may be round-nosed, sharp-nosed, cylindrical or hollow-pointed so that they expand on impact. Such bullets are not suitable for high-velocity weapons such as military rifles and automatic pistols, however. These weapons use bullets with a lead or steel core that is wholly or partially enclosed in a jacket made of aluminum or alloys of copper with zinc or nickel.

Shotgun cartridges are larger versions of rifle and pistol cartridges and consist of a charge, a case and a primer cap. Instead of a bullet, the front end of the cartridge is sealed by a wad, a disk of closely packed cardboard, and a plastic body filled with small shotgun pellets. Crimped cardboard holds the pellets in place. Some shotgun cartridges, intended for shooting at large animals such as deer or bears, are fitted with solid, large-caliber bullets.

Gunshot wound evidence

Forensic examiners carefully examine the wounds of gunshot victims. The appearance of the wound depends on the range at which the weapon was fired. Establishing the range is important in helping investigators to determine exactly what happened. For example, a case of apparent suicide would look highly doubtful if the evidence showed the gun had been fired from farther than arm's length from the victim's body. Equally, self-defense may be easier to prove if the evidence shows that the gun was shot at close range, when discharging the weapon might have been the user's last line of defense.

In cases where victim and assailant are at close quarters, and particularly where they are struggling, the gun may be fired with the muzzle pressing against the victim's body. In such cases, the discharge of the cartridge produces hot gases and soot particles that are driven into the skin and cause burning at the edges of the wound. If the wound was made through clothing, then the fibers around the hole in the cloth made by the bullet may be scorched by the heat of the discharge. The material may show a star-shaped tear pattern around the bullet hole.

What signs on the body indicate a weapon was fired from a slightly longer range? Particles of unburned and partly-burned powder are driven into the skin, causing a pattern called "tattooing." If the victim was alive when the wound was inflicted, the tattooing is usually orange or brown in color, but if the wound was inflicted when the victim was already dead, then the color is a more subdued gray-yellow.

To make the most accurate estimation of the range, a ballistics examiner usually fires the suspect weapon from varying distances into cloth or fabric that matches the victim's clothing as closely as possible. The range that leaves the pattern most like that on the victim's clothing, given identical ammunition, is then the most probable range at which the shot was fired.

BELOW Using a laser beam to determine the precise path taken by a bullet.

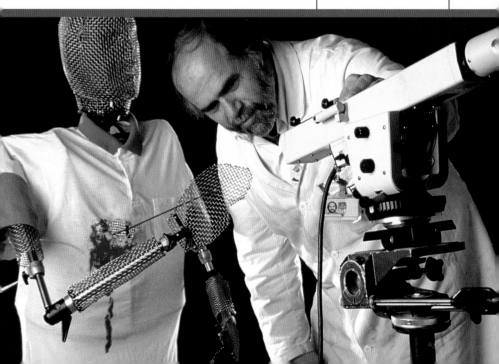

THE KENNEDY INVESTIGATION:

one marksman or two?

For years after President John F. Kennedy was assassinated in **1963**, rumors persisted that more than one marksman had taken part in the shooting. In **November 1977**, investigators decided to subject the fragments recovered from the car to neutron activation analysis. This involves bombarding an object with neutrons, which renders it radioactive because the neutrons are captured by the atoms that make up the object's structure. These atoms then begin emitting gamma rays, which can be measured and analyzed to reveal traces of all the elements present.

John F. Kennedy

Some of the bullet fragments recovered from the scene were found in the President's body, others in Governor John Connolly's wrist, and the remainder in the car. One complete bullet was found on Connolly's stretcher at the hospital. Analysis of the precise chemical composition of the fragments showed they were pieces of only two bullets: one had fatally wounded the President; the other had passed through the governor's wrist. Though the bullets differed slightly in their composition, experts found that they had almost certainly been fired from the same gun. No fragments were found of the bullets that wounded both the President and the governor in the back.

Though the evidence did not prove conclusively that Lee Harvey Oswald had acted alone, it also did not support theories about other marksmen firing from different locations. Unfortunately, an opportunity for more definite conclusions had been lost at the time of the autopsy. On security grounds, the FBI refused access to the specialist photographer assigned to take pictures of the gunshot wounds. Instead, an FBI photographer was used and the resulting photographs were deficient. They did not identify the different entry and exit wounds, provide a scale to indicate their size, or clearly show the internal organs. The evidence thus remains inconclusive and, without hard facts, conspiracy theories continue to flourish.

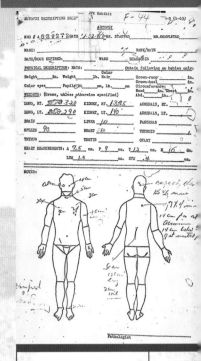

ABOVE The autopsy description, included as an exhibit for the House Assassinations Committee formed in 1976.

LEFT A detective carries the 7.65 Mannlicher-Carcano rifle believed to have been used to kill the President, which was found on the fifth floor of the Dallas building from which the shots were fired.

BACKGROUND PICTURE Kennedy slumps after being shot in the open White House car.

The tragic turret on

USS IOWA

During a firing drill on the battleship USS Iowa on April 19, 1989, five bags of the explosive being loaded into the center gun of number two turret of the ship exploded without warning. Forty-seven seamen, including the entire crew of the armored turret, were killed.

A Navy investigation concluded that the explosion had been caused by sabotage on the part of the petty officer in charge of the gun turret. They believed the officer intended to commit suicide and also kill a former friend working at the bottom level of the turret. Both men died in the explosion, but their families harshly criticized the Navy's findings.

The Senate Armed Services Committee decided to commission explosives experts at Sandia National Laboratories to conduct a full technical investigation. When they checked the drill used to load the gun, the experts found that once the shell was placed in the barrel, the bags of explosives were pushed slowly up the barrel by a power-operated rammer until they were close to, but not in contact with, the shell. On the day of the exercise, the left gun was loaded in 44 seconds and the right gun in 61 seconds.

Naval investigators claimed that analysis of debris in the gun-barrel showed traces of steel wool, brake fluid and calcium hypochlorite. They insisted that

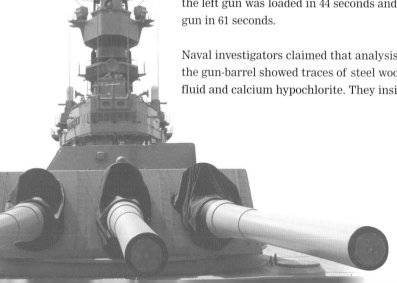

this had been deliberately placed in the barrel as an incendiary device and had set off the charges when the pressure of the rammer was applied. The Sandia experts analyzed the traces and found they were made up of steel fibers, calcium and chlorine. But these elements were also found in the other gun turrets of the USS Iowa, as well as in the turrets of her sister ships, USS Wisconsin and USS New Jersey. Traces of these elements were found in lubricants and cleaning fluids used in the gun turrets, and in some cases were also found in sea water.

If the Navy was wrong in concluding that the explosion was a deliberate attempt at sabotage and suicide, then what had really caused the disaster? Examiners found that the rammer on the center gun was pushing the explosive bags two feet farther up the barrel than it should have done. Other evidence suggested that the sailor controlling the rammer had been inexperienced and had operated the rammer much too quickly. Both these factors may have caused the explosives to be slammed against the bulk of the shell with some force, but tests showed that such action did not detonate them. Then investigators discovered that extra sticks of explosive had been arranged in a loose layer at the top of each bag to make up the weight, and this would have imposed the additional stress necessary to cause the explosion.

When tests were carried out by dropping a steel weight representing the rammer onto bags of explosive containing a loose top layer, the bags exploded. As a result of these findings, the Navy was able to change the loading procedure and ensure that such an accident could not happen again. Had the explosion been ascribed to sabotage, more sailors might have died in similar circumstances.

ABOVE Crew members fighting the fire after number two turret exploded.

OPPOSITE TOP Bodies of the gun turret crew at a ceremony at Dover AFB, Delaware.

OPPOSITE BOTTOM Gun turrets of the USS Iowa—number two turret is in the background with its guns trained out to the side.

THE FLAMES OF DESTRUCTION: FIRE AND EXPLOSIVES

Criminals harness the terrible power of fire and explosives both to achieve their aims directly and to disguise crimes they have committed using other means. Buildings and property are deliberately destroyed for insurance fraud; letter bombs and remote-control devices eliminate specific targets; and evidence of violence and theft are burned in the hope of destroying all possible links with the perpetrator. Nevertheless, as forensic examiners gain new and more effective detection methods, criminals find it much harder to get away with these kinds of activities.

RIGHT Remains of a house totally wrecked by a gas explosion.

Accident or arson?

In any case of death apparently resulting from fire, a crucial goal of the forensic examination is to determine what caused the fire. If a victim's body has been burned in an effort to conceal a murder, for example, there is usually evidence to show someone started the fire deliberately. Alternatively, the perpetrator may have started the fire in order to file a fraudulent insurance claim, to destroy evidence of fraud, even to get rid of a business rival. Or, it may simply have been started to gratify the psychological urges of a pyromaniac.

In most cases, setting a fire requires using some kind of accelerant that helps the flames take hold. Fires tend to spread upward as well as outward, so the search for the start-point is usually focused on

ABOVE A horrific fire at King's Cross subway station in London in 1987, which killed 31 people, was thought to have been started by a carelessly dropped cigarette igniting an old wooden escalator. In a reconstruction, the flames, which can just be seen then spread to engulf the whole escalator. Within minutes, the wooden framework of the escalator was fully ablaze, preventing the trapped passengers using it as an escape route to the surface.

LEFT The pattern of smoke on the wall of a room can help to show where a fire started and how it spread.

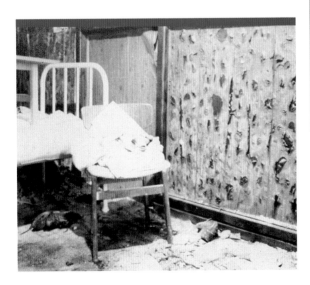

**RIGHT Fire spreads
upward from a start-point
in an apartment block.**

the lowest point of the burned-out area. Investigators
may find traces of gasoline or other flammable
hydrocarbons, either lingering in the air or present
in fabrics or surfaces on the edge of the area.
Laboratory analysis can identify these accelerants.

Piles of ash at the base of a fire may show where
an arsonist piled material before lighting it. The
presence of more than one point of origin is another
compelling sign that a blaze is no accident. Likewise,
evidence of breaking and entering can point to
arson. Where appropriate, investigators can check to
see whether security or sprinkler systems have been
deliberately disabled. If they suspect fraud or

insurance swindles, they search the premises carefully for the remains of goods or burned documents.

Where a fire is genuinely accidental, the cause is usually all too clear. It might be faulty electrical wiring in the building, a gas leak, or a lighted cigarette that was carelessly disposed. In other cases, evidence of a lightning strike or the presence of volatile materials stored near natural heat sources may show how the fire began.

Explosive evidence

Explosions are caused by a combination of materials which, when detonated, set off a fast-burning reaction that produces gas. The gas causes the pressure inside the bomb's container to rise rapidly until the casing bursts and the pieces are blasted outward at high speed. These fast-moving pieces combine with the blast effect of the expanding gases that are suddenly released and travel at speeds of up to 7,000 miles per hour, leading to damage and casualties.

Most criminals who use explosives–excluding large, well-funded terrorist groups–make their own

BELOW Part of the bomb used to destroy the PanAm Boeing Flight 103 747 over Lockerbie, Scotland in 1988.

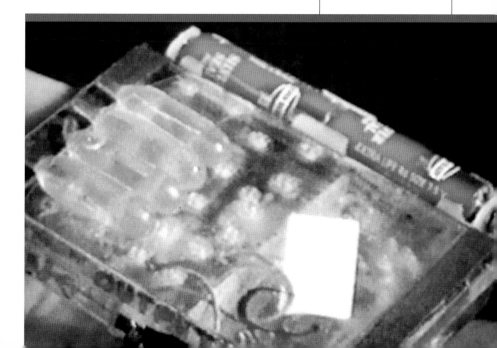

incendiary devices. The majority of these homemade explosives are low explosives, made from ingredients that are relatively easy to obtain. One traditional mixture, a black powder once used in muskets and pistols, includes a combination of charcoal, sulfur and potassium or sodium nitrate. Others contain the essential combination of a fuel and an oxidant using ingredients as familiar as sugar and weed killer.

Powerful explosives, such as dynamite, TNT or RDX, are inert by themselves, and can be handled and even set on fire without exploding. To set them

Sabotage

Forensic Fact

In vehicle sabotage cases, the criminal may have used saws and wire cutters, which will leave their own signature marks on the material being cut. Even knife scratches can give key evidence, especially if investigators find the suspect item and can use it to produce a test mark for comparison purposes. The pattern of marks that occur when the tool is manufactured, together with any nicks and scratches it has acquired since then, can help enormously in confirming its origin and history.

Wreckage in the aftermath of an Italian terrorist killing with a car bomb.

off, a primer—a small charge of an explosive that is even more sensitive to heat or shock—is needed. Primer charges are usually detonated by blasting caps, which are triggered by lighting a safety fuse or applying an electric current. If investigators find the remains of one of these caps at the scene, they usually assume that someone deliberately carried out the explosion.

Examining the debris

Forensic examiners can uncover a great deal of information about an explosion by studying the site of the blast and analyzing the debris. In most cases, an explosion leaves a crater at the center of the blast, and examiners remove debris from this area for further tests. Fragments of softer materials such as wood, rubber or insulation may have absorbed traces of the explosives. Harder materials, such as metals, may have traces deposited on their surfaces. A vacuum pump collects vapors from suspect surfaces and passes them through its own high-speed gas chromatography equipment to identify their components. The device can detect commercial and military explosives, including the more sophisticated types of plastic explosives.

Detonators provide still more evidence and are sometimes linked to a battery through a device set to trigger the circuit. This might be an alarm clock, which allows the bomb to be set to go off at a particular time, or a mercury tilt switch, so that if the device is moved the circuit is completed and the bomb goes off. Many car bombs are wired to the vehicle's ignition, so the act of trying to start the engine sets off the explosion.

BELOW Searching through the wreckage left when an El Al Boeing 747 freighter crashed into a block of flats near Amsterdam's Schiphol airport on October 4, 1992, a disaster that was eventually found to be caused by metal fatigue in the aircraft's mountings.

STEVEN BENSON

a family destroyed

Steven Benson came from a wealthy Florida family and expected to inherit millions of dollars when his older relatives died. On the morning of July 9, 1985, he arrived at his grandmother's home in Naples, Florida, to pick up some equipment to mark out a site for a new home. He loaded the family car, a 1978 Chevrolet Suburban, with stakes and plans, and, just before 9:00 AM, he and his mother, sister and adopted brother Scott went out to the car, ready to drive to the site. Saying that he had forgotten his tape measure, Steven threw the car keys to Scott and went back into the house. Scott climbed into the driver's seat. As he turned the ignition key, the car exploded in two separate but devastating blasts. Steven and his sister Carol Lynn were the only survivors.

ABOVE Steven Benson at his trial in 1986.

RIGHT Aerial view of the crime scene, with the wreckage in front of the Benson house in Naples, Florida.

While searching the wreckage, forensic investigators found the remains of a bomb that had been made from a length of galvanized metal pipe, threaded at both ends and sealed with end-caps. One of the end-caps carried the letter "G" for its maker, Grinnell, and the other bore a "U" for Union Brand. Close to the site of the explosion, they discovered fragments of four 1.5-volt batteries together with a manual switch and a piece of circuit board that was not part of the car's electrical system.

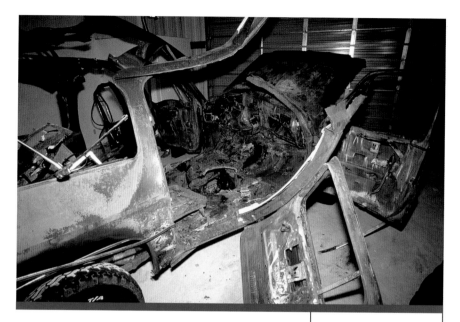

ABOVE AND BELOW The twisted wreckage of the Chevrolet where Steven Benson's mother and brother died.

Teams of investigators visited local hardware stores, junkyards and construction sites to check the sources of the pipes and end-caps. One store had sold two Union Brand end-caps four days before the explosion, and the description of the customer–a tall, heavily-built man–fit that of Steven Benson. When sales tickets for the components were chemically treated, they revealed Steven Benson's palm print, proving that he had bought the bomb-making equipment.

ABOVE AND BELOW The twisted wreckage of the Chevrolet where Steven Benson's mother and brother died.

On August 21, 1985, six weeks and a day after the deadly explosion, Benson was arrested. Almost a year later he was found guilty of murdering his mother and brother. The evidence revealed that Steven Benson had been stealing from his mother for some time. Having found him out, she was about to amend her will so that Steven would not inherit the ten million dollars he had been expecting. To avoid losing his inheritance, he had been willing to literally blow his family apart.

The double tragedies of the

WORLD TRADE CENTER

On February 23, 1993, a yellow van was parked in the underground garage of the northernmost tower of New York's World Trade Center. It contained a massive bomb that, when detonated, killed six people and injured more than a thousand. Damage to the tower reached five hundred million dollars.

Specialists from the FBI's Materials and Documents Unit scoured the crime scene and managed to isolate trace evidence of urea nitrate. From the extent of the damage, they were sure that at least 1,200 pounds of the explosive was used.

ABOVE Investigators examine the rubble in the basement of the World Trade Center.

LEFT The conspirators hoped that one of the Center's twin towers would collapse, bringing down the other, with a much greater loss of life.

Agents hunting for the bombers got an early break when an immigrant named Mohammad Salameh called at the rental office to claim back his $400 deposit on the rented Ryder van used in the bombing. Salameh claimed the van had been stolen from him the day before by Ramizi Ahmed Yousef, one of the principal conspirators. The investigation led police to a Jersey City apartment and a nearby storage shed that Yousef used as a bomb factory. There they found Salameh's fingerprints on bomb-making chemicals.

The fingerprints of Yousef and his chief conspirator, Eyad Izmoil, were also found on chemicals and on bomb-making manuals at the site. However, both men had left the United States on a flight from Kennedy Airport right after the bombing. The FBI posted a $2 million reward, and two years later Yousef was arrested in Pakistan, after earlier sightings in Manila and Bangkok, then extradited to the United States to stand trial. Izmiol was later arrested in Jordan, and in November 1997 the two men were put on trial together with their fellow plotters.

Six men with links to Arab countries were eventually convicted of conspiracy to carry out the bombing, which was intended to punish the United States for its continued support of Israel. They had hoped to cause far more destruction by blowing up one tower completely so that it toppled onto the other. All six conspirators were sentenced to life imprisonment.

GROUND ZERO

On September 11, 2001 the two 110-story towers of the World Trade Center that stood tall as a monument to Western democracy and economic power were again targeted by terrorists. In this new and more lethal attack, the towers were erased from the Manhattan skyline.

It began at 8:45 AM when American Airlines flight 11, bound for Los Angeles, hit the North Tower with devastating impact and instant loss of life. The horror of this first tragedy was barely realized when United Airlines flight 175, also bound for Los Angeles, hit the South Tower at 9:03 AM. Clearly, this was no accident.

Since the airliners had just taken off, they were full of fuel, which intensified the explosion and caused fatal damage to the structure of the buildings. Within less than two hours, both towers collapsed, releasing huge amounts of smoke and debris. The New York Fire Department was quick to take up the challenge. Many firefighters died in heroic efforts to save as many people as possible from the collapsing buildings, and afterward, from the chaos, dust and falling debris in the area. Hospitals were put on alert and, as Ground Zero began to emerge, a massive search for survivors began. Specially trained dogs were used to pinpoint buried casualties, but very few were found alive.

Efforts were then focused on identifying the thousands who had perished. The nature of this disaster created huge identification problems and a multidisciplinary effort was launched to perform forensic pathology, forensic odontology, anthropology, photography and DNA services, a process in which dentists and dental forensics play particularly important roles. Those victims who could not be identified visually or by paper-

identification were sent to the dental examiner's station. The American Dental Association (ADA) officials assigned up to 30 members to work in four-hour shifts around the clock. Typically, in bomb or explosive events, about 80 percent of the positive identifications will be done based on the victims' dental records. This level of accuracy is possible because teeth are the hardest substance in the body. Although teeth are susceptible to natural forces of decay, they cannot be destroyed by external forces including fires, floods or explosives. Technology, such as digital X-rays, forensic computer programs and federal databases can also facilitate the operation to identify the victims and help bring closure to their relatives and friends. But despite the efforts of numerous forensic experts, the total death toll at Ground Zero may never be known.

ABOVE Firefighters work at the site known as Ground Zero, where the twin towers once stood. The work of forensic examiners was focused here on identifying the thousands who died in the attack.

OPPOSITE The north World Trade Center tower shows a gaping hole where the first airliner collided with it, as the south tower explodes in a fireball when struck by the second aircraft.

UNMASKING THE CRIMINAL: FRAUDS AND FORGERIES

Forensic scientists are increasingly being asked to examine and test various documents in order to help identify criminals or prove acts of forgery or counterfeiting. Even fragments of writing can reveal numerous clues about a criminal's identity. Evidence might come from personal letters or ransom demands, or printed documents ranging from pawnbroker's receipts to airline or train tickets.

A sign of the crimes

Experts have devised several ways to check suspect signatures. By putting a sheet of tracing paper over a signature and marking the tops (or the bottoms) of each letter and then joining them up, they produce a zigzag line. Different authentic examples of the same signature all show a very similar line but a forgery, even one that seems convincing at first glance, often shows quite a different zigzag pattern from the original.

The baseline of the writing is another key indicator. For example, Abraham Lincoln's distinctive signature featured a stepped baseline in which the initial "A" and the final "ln" lay on different levels from the rest of the name–an idiosyncrasy that several would-be forgers of Lincoln's day missed.

Abraham Lincoln and his genuine signature, showing the characteristic three steps of the baseline, a feature often missed by forgers.

In other cases criminals try to profit by passing off as genuine forged or altered letters, bank drafts, checks and similar financial documents. Investigators can check watermarks and signatures to identify forgeries. They can also identify minute characteristics unique to individual typewriters or printers in pieces of text to help investigators get a head start locating the machine the perpetrator used.

ABOVE Testing a US currency bill under fluorescent light to reveal evidence of forgery.

BELOW Researchers working on a computerized system for handwriting recognition.

Revealing the criminal's hand

Handwriting experts study individual variations from the standard writing styles, especially any differences that may be characteristic of the writer, since these will help the most to identify him or her. For example, the letter "i" may be not be dotted, may be written without an upstroke, or may have one or more small "eyelets" where the movement of the pen changed direction while forming the letter.

Experts also scrutinize the proportion or relative height of different letters. Of course, variations do occur even in an individual's ordinary handwriting, but certain established ratios are usually consistent. For example, the ratio between the part of the letter "g" above the line to the overall height of the letter tends to remain the same in an individual writer, regardless of the person's writing style.

The overall slant of the writing from the vertical is another fairly consistent factor. This can range from thirty-five degrees to the right to as much as fifty degrees to the left in different styles, but it should be more or less consistent for each person's hand. Writers' styles also differ in the spacing of individual letters, words and lines. In particular, a signature or a complete line of text tends to follow a consistent path for an individual. The baseline is either straight and level or angled or curved upward or downward or both. Another common individual variation is the presence or absence of connectors– the strokes that join letters in handwritten words.

An inky disguise

Some crimes do not involve imitating another person's handwriting. Instead, criminals try to disguise their own writing to avoid revealing their identity. The would-be forger often tries to fool people by changing the direction in which the letters

A checkered past

Forensic Fact

Instead of attempting a forgery, many criminals alter existing documents such as checks and bank drafts, either by changing the name of the payee or by increasing the amount involved. They may erase

one or more characters on the existing document by scratching away the surface layer of the paper, then typing or writing over the alteration. However, microscopic analysis usually reveals the signs of such erasures by lighting one side of the document to highlight changes in the surface layers. Criminals also use chemical agents to remove existing characters. But, when examined under infrared or ultraviolet lighting, the part of the paper that was treated with chemicals reveals the truth.

A forged check has an additional figure added to it by a forger using a different pen from the original.

slant, changing the size of the letters, printing in block capitals, or even writing with the other hand. Writing quickly or slowly, deliberately misspelling words, or trying to copy another handwriting style are more familiar tricks of the trade.

One way to confirm the writer's identity is to locate the source of the document in question. A search of a suspect's home or office may uncover partially destroyed rough drafts; an examination of the remaining pages of a notepad or the desk blotter may show pressure marks made by the pen used to write the document. Examiners can reassemble fragments of torn-up and burned documents, then read them by photographing them under infrared light. When an imprint remains on paper that was underneath the document when it was written (for example, in the successive pages of a notepad), electrostatic detection offers the answers. Experts tear off several pages from the pad in succession then use electrostatic detection to retrieve the images left by the pressure of the pen or pencil.

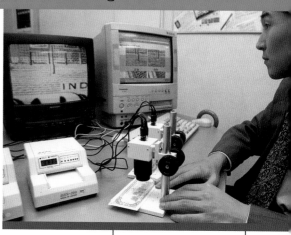

ABOVE A Japanese machine is used for identifying forged currency using ultraviolet light and magnetic sensors.

Mechanical signatures

Forensic examiners have faced new challenges in detecting the origins of machine-written documents since typewriters and computer printers came into use. Manual typewriter text analysis is based on the fact that different pressures on the keys and differing wear on individual keys eventually build up a series of variations. These features can be detected in text typed on a particular machine.

Advances in typing and printing technology have tended to make this kind of analysis less useful. For example, with electric typewriters, even pressure is applied to all the key strokes. This reduces variations in the weight with which different letters are pressed. Even so, faults in the mechanism can create new inconsistencies, much like the action of a typist's fingers on a mechanical typewriter.

The advent of computer-controlled printers has posed the greatest obstacle to examiners seeking those quirks and variations that identify a particular machine. In the first word-processors, output was often delivered on a daisy-wheel printer, where the type was set on bars that formed the spokes of a wheel. These were susceptible to wear and tear in a similar way to typewriters, and because the mechanisms of both golf-ball and daisy-wheel machines can become slightly misaligned with use, documents printed on a particular machine could still be identified with some accuracy.

Since then, ink-jet, bubble-jet, and laser printers have become more widespread and this has tended to eliminate such inconsistencies. Experts have sought other ways of linking the author to the document, such as tracing the original word-processor files on the hard disk of the computer. Although the writer may have carefully deleted the files in question, computer experts who know how and where to search for these files can often retrieve them.

BELOW Testing inks using chromatography to reveal their exact composition.

A watermark to dye for

Elaborate forgeries of printed documents can be extremely convincing at first glance. However, they are often revealed as counterfeit when experts test the paper or the ink. Modern inks fall into four basic types: black inks; India ink or carbon-black ink; colored inks; inks made with synthetic dyes. Spectrometry and thin-layer chromatography are two of the methods used to isolate each type of ink.

Paper, too, can be classified based on the way it was manufactured. Certain papers have particular watermarks. Others are made from synthetic fibers or have optical brightening agents

25. Sept. 1988.

Dear Boss

I keep on hearing the police have caught me but they wont fix me just yet. I have laughed when they look so clever and talk about being on the right track. That joke about Leather apron gave me real fits. I am down on whores and I shant quit ripping them till I do get buckled. Grand work the last job was. I gave the lady no time to squeal. How can they catch me now. I love my work and want to start again. You will soon hear of me with my funny little games. I saved some of the proper red stuff in a ginger beer bottle over the last job to write with but it went thick like glue and I cant use it. Red ink is fit enough I hope ha. ha. The next job I do I shall clip the ladys ears off and send to the police officers just for jolly wouldnt you. Keep this letter back till I do a bit more work then give it out straight My knifes so nice and sharp I want to get to work right away if I get a chance. Good luck.

yours truly

Jack the Ripper

Dont mind me giving the trade name

like fluorocarbons that are added to make them whiter and less transparent for high-quality color printing. Papers also differ in terms of the surface treatment used to prepare them for printing. Some are hot-rolled, while others are treated with sizing materials, synthetic resins or starch.

When specialists can pinpoint the date when a particular paper or type of ink was originally introduced, they can expose an otherwise convincing historical document as a forgery.

Some forgers try to increase the value of postage stamps to collectors by faking the cancellation stamps, and many attempt the toughest forgeries of all by producing counterfeit currency. Here, they face huge obstacles because mints use papers and printed designs chosen specifically to make forgery as difficult as possible. Even where the reproduction of the printed design looks perfect to the naked eye, techniques such as microspectrophotometry can distinguish between genuine and forged notes (bills). These methods clearly reveal the absorption spectrum of the ink used in individual printed lines, thus separating the real from the fake.

THE HITLER DIARIES

In 1981, the German publishing firm, Grüner and Jahr, paid a sum equivalent to two million dollars for 27 volumes of handwritten text believed to be the diaries of Adolf Hitler, along with a previously undiscovered third volume of Hitler's Mein Kampf. Supposedly, these volumes had been smuggled out of Berlin in the last days of World War Two, but the airplane carrying them had crashed in what was later Communist East Germany. The papers had fallen into the hands of a collector who had brought the documents to Gerd Heidemann, a journalist on the staff of the German news magazine *Stern*, which was also published by Grüner and Jahr.

ABOVE Konrad Kujau, the forger of the diaries, appearing in court with samples of his handiwork.

Naturally, the documents were compared with known samples of Hitler's handwriting to determine if they were authentic. Two experts were brought in to perform this task: Max Frei-Sultzer, former head of the Zürich police forensic science department, and Ordway Hilton, a specialist in document verification from Landrum in South Carolina. Together with another German police documents expert, both men confirmed that the texts had been written by the same person, which turned out to be true. The diaries were not authentic, however–they had been forged by a small-time criminal named Konrad Kujau, who had also managed to forge the sample used to check the diaries' authorship!

Forensic tests by the West German police and government revealed the truth. Instead of checking the handwriting, they focused on the paper and ink used in the diaries. After testing the paper under ultraviolet light, they found it contained a whitening agent that had first been introduced in 1954. The

Mein Kampf

threads attaching the official-looking seals to the volumes contained viscose and polyester, materials that were also developed after the war. In addition, none of the four different types of ink used had been available when the diaries were supposedly written. Finally, a test involving the evaporation of chloride from the ink was done to find out how long the ink had been on the paper. The results showed that the so-called "Hitler diaries" had been written less than a year before the tests were carried out. Once again, forensic science had distinguished fact from fiction.

ABOVE Hitler's dedication and signature on a first edition of the book.

BACKGROUND The Remington typewriter on which Hitler had written Mein Kampf.

BELOW At a press conference, Gerd Heidemann denies that he had set out to cheat *Stern* magazine with the forged diaries.

CRIMINAL TRACES

Is it possible to commit a crime without leaving a trace? Forensic science is based on the assumption that a person who is present at that location exchanges trace evidence with the scene in many different ways. Traces may be found at the crime scene that can be linked to a suspect, just as traces found on the suspect may link him or her to the scene–or indeed to the crime itself. Hairs, fibers, particles of dust or soil, plant debris, paint flakes and other microscopic evidence can trap even the most careful criminals and prove they were involved in their meticulously planned crimes. Likewise, fingerprints and footprints can help experts positively identify an individual victim or criminal, and also prove that a suspect was present at the scene of a crime. Even a microscopic bit of evidence can defeat a criminal.

Criminal colors

A single flake of paint may provide a great deal of information. The shape, color or chemical constituents of the paint can be matched with the surface from which it was taken. Paint samples are particularly important in cases involving vehicles,

LEFT Cross sections of different samples of red paint and underlying layers from different red automobiles.

RIGHT Cross sections of red household paint.

and forensic laboratories maintain large databases listing the precise compositions and ranges of colors used by the larger manufacturers. Using a microscope, experts can compare the colors. They can also break down the polymer binder that holds each layer together and analyze it by pyrolysis gas chromatography, where the paint chips are heated to release their constituents in gaseous form. This effectively creates a single "fingerprint" for each layer and helps to establish points of comparison with other samples.

Hair-raising stories

Criminal or animal? Victim or clothing? Whatever their origin, hairs provide useful evidence because they retain their structure for a long time, due to the tough outer covering of the cuticle. Using microscope technology, examiners can tell whether a hair has been artificially bleached or colored. By looking at where the colored or bleached zone ends relative to the root of the hair, they can estimate when the last coloring or bleaching was done.

A person's hairs also can sometimes reveal the presence of poison in the body. In cases of drug abuse or arsenic poisoning, the part of the hair in which these traces are found can indicate when doses were administered.

Further information can be gathered through neutron activation analysis, where a hair is bombarded with neutrons in the core of a nuclear reactor. The neutrons collide with the atoms of the different trace elements in the sample and make

ABOVE Photomicrograph of a human hair, magnified 1,200 times.

TOP Preparing a hair sample for microscopic analysis.

TOP LEFT Individual identifier–a false-color computer graphics image of a human fingerprint.

them radioactive. By measuring the resulting gamma radiation, experts can measure the most minute traces of every constituent of the sample. More recently, the use of hair as a source for producing samples of a subject's DNA has replaced this powerful but fairly tedious technique (see Chapter 12).

Shreds of evidence

All fibers used in clothing and furnishing fabrics are natural, man-made, or a combination of the two. Natural fibers include wool and silk, vegetable fibers like cotton, hemp, sisal, flax (used in making linen) and jute; a wide range of animal hairs such as cashmere, camel hair, mohair and alpaca; and furs like mink or sable. Each one has a characteristic appearance that enables experts to distinguish them from human and other animal hairs under microscopic examination. A fiber can be identified by pinpointing its precise diameter, its exact color, and other distinguishing features such as striations running along the fibers from the production process. Tests may turn up particles of agents such as titanium dioxide, which is added during manufacture to change the fabric's texture and surface.

A very accurate technique called microspectrophotometry can compare the colors of fibers, even when only small fragments have been retrieved. This involves shining a beam of visible or infrared light on a sample of the fiber under a microscope to display the absorption spectrum of the fiber on a computer screen. Chromatography can also be used to separate the individual chemicals used to make the dye by dissolving the dye in a suitable solution.

Shattering clues

Samples of glass from vehicle windows or headlights, or from windows or glassware at the crime scene, can provide important evidence. Large fragments of glass can sometimes be fitted into the lamp or

ABOVE, TOP TO BOTTOM
Synthetic fibers, showing detectable differences in structure: acetate, nylon, and vivrelle.

Dust clouds

Forensic Fact

Particles of dust picked up at the crime scene or on a suspect's clothing can reveal important clues. Soil from gardens, open land, tracks or woodland can contain plant spores, pollen particles, insects and micro-organisms, and microscopic analysis can reveal all of these substances and help to indicate a likely source. Other dust particles of flour, concrete, coal or brick, for example, can suggest a person's occupation or lead investigators to his or her workplace.

Color-scanning electron microscope image of household dust, made up of particles of soil and sand, skin scales, household fibers, and pet hair.

LEFT Bullet holes in a glass window producing radial and concentric fractures, where the intersections reveal the order in which the shots struck the glass.

ABOVE False-color scanning electron micrograph of glass fibers.

BELOW Fingerprint classifications including different types of loops and arches.

Plain whorl

Double loop

Double loop

Accidental

Plain arch

Tented arch

Tented arch

Radial loop

Ulnar loop

Central pocket loop

window pane from which they were broken for a positive match, or the glass can actually preserve a record of the order in which events happened. When a series of gunshots pierce a window pane, for example, the first shot makes a hole surrounded by a set of radial fractures. These, in turn, are linked by concentric fractures. The stress marks along the cross sections of these fracture patterns can tell forensic examiners which side of the glass was hit first. Developing fractures stop at the point of any existing fracture lines, so the fractures radiating from a second bullet hole end where they meet the radial fractures from the first. A third bullet hole produces fractures that terminate where they meet fractures radiating from the first two holes, and so on.

Different types of glass have different densities and refractive indices, both of which scientists can measure. Although a particular combination of density and refractive index is rarely unique, the FBI laboratory maintains data that shows how often any individual combination is likely to be found. If two samples with the same properties come from a relatively rare type of glass, this increases their importance as evidence.

Fingerprint families

For at least 3,000 years, people have recognized that each human fingerprint is unique. Complex ridge patterns are different in every single individual's prints. The general arrangement of the ridges follows a series of recognizable patterns. This means prints can be classified so that the search for a match can begin with general characteristics, then proceed to more detailed points of similarity.

Two-thirds of the human population, for example, have ridge patterns that form loops. These are classified as "radial" (from the radius bone of the forearm) if the loops open toward the little-finger side of the hand; "ulnar" (from the ulna bone) if they open toward the thumb. The center of the loop is called the core. The "delta" is the triangular pattern where the outermost looped ridge lines meet the horizontal ridge-line pattern running across the base of the fingertip.

Almost one-third of the population has ridge patterns in whorls, which can be further split into plain whorls, double loops, central-pocket loops and accidental loops. About one person in 20 has ridge patterns arranged in arches, which are described as plain arches if they follow a smooth, wavelike pattern. If they end in a sharper point at the center, they are called tented arches.

To simplify fingerprint searches, Henry's system, and the FBI's later version of this system, splits the variations into 1,024 coded groups. Analysts give an individual's ten prints a numerical value. The fingerprints are arranged as a double row in sequence: Right index Right ring Left thumb Left middle Left little Right thumb Right middle Right little Left index. Each print is given a value depending on the pattern of the print and the finger in question. If either of the fingers at the beginning of each row (right index or the right thumb) has a whorl pattern, it scores 16. If either finger of the second pair (the right ring or the right middle) has a whorl, it scores eight. The third, fourth and last pairs score four, two and one respectively if either of them has a whorl. Any finger that has no whorl pattern is given zero.

The scores on each row are then added up and one further point added to each row, unless all the fingers on that row have whorls. The result is presented as a fraction, such as 14/8 or 16/9. This provides an overall class figure, which analysts use as a starting point in their search for a matching print.

This type of pattern recognition is an ideal application for computers. They can scan and store a given fingerprint as a digital pattern, taking into account the type and location on the print of each individual feature. These automated fingerprint identification systems (A.F.I.S.) can be sent across the world to be compared or matched with prints obtained by local officials.

ABOVE An ultraviolet light source is used to make latent fingerprints stand out against brightly colored or patterned surfaces after dusting them with fluorescent powder.

ABOVE A fiberglass latent print brush (top) and latent print-lifting tape (bottom).

A helping hand

Forensic Fact

The patterns of the ridged skin on the palms of the hands and the soles of the feet are unique to each individual. If a barefoot print or a palm print is retrieved at the scene of a crime, potential suspects whose prints do not match can be eliminated. In some countries, the barefoot prints of newborns are used to provide positive proof of individual identity in maternity hospitals, since babies' fingerprints are too small to easily identify their features.

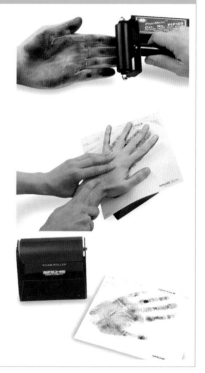

Inking a subject's palm (top), rolling the palm on to the record card (center), and the finished palm (bottom) showing clear ridge details.

Revealing and recording prints

The fingerprints investigators gather at crime scenes fall into three categories: visible, plastic or latent. Visible prints are those made by fingers that have been in contact with a marker such as wet paint, ink or blood. Plastic prints are made by the fingers pressing on a material like soap, wax or putty which retains the image of the finger-tip ridges. Latent prints, the most common type, are also the hardest to see and need to be exposed before examination.

Latent fingerprints are made when the natural oils and perspiration present between the fingertip ridges are transferred to a surface by touch. Examiners use different methods to reveal such minute traces, depending on the type of surface being tested. Hard and non-absorbent surfaces like glass, painted wood, tiles or metal are usually dusted with fingerprint powder, which sticks to the traces of oil and perspiration left by the fingertip.

Chemical methods are used to pick up fingerprint evidence from soft or porous surfaces such as cloth or paper. One of the latest techniques for revealing latent prints involves illuminating them with laser light, which causes chemicals in human perspiration to fluoresce in darkness. In all these cases, the prints have to be placed on permanent record by being photographed or "lifted" using adhesive tape or plastic sheet to attract the fingerprint powder and preserve the all-important patterns.

Fingerprinting the dead

Fingerprinting has now become a standard part of autopsy procedure, conducted after all other possible trace evidence has been removed from the fingertips and fingernails. If time has passed since the victim's death, examiners may undertake "reconstructive" procedures to obtain a clear set of prints.

Fingerprints are usually taken from dead bodies when *rigor mortis* has passed off and after the body has been kept in cold storage. Sometimes, when bodies are badly decomposed, the hands, or occasionally individual fingers, must be removed in order to take the prints. Mummified bodies may need to have the fingertips softened by soaking them in a mixture of glycol, lactic acid and distilled water, sometimes for several weeks, before prints can be taken.

BELOW Taking the fingerprints of a corpse.

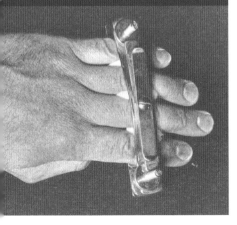

The most difficult subjects are those in which the skin has been softened by dampness or immersion in water. In some cases, glycerine or liquid wax has to be injected into the fingertip from below the joint. If the damage to the tissues is more extensive, the skin can be stripped away from the hand, then mounted on a surgical glove in order to obtain prints.

HIGH FIBER

Between 1979 and 1981 a series of brutal stranglings of young men terrorized communities in the city of Atlanta, Georgia. Almost the only forensic evidence linking the killings was a peculiar type of fiber found on the victims' clothing. This fiber had an unusual, triple-lobed cross-section that appeared to correspond with fibers used in rugs or carpets. Unfortunately, police were unable to track down the maker of the fiber. When newspapers mentioned the fiber evidence in February 1981, the killer changed his methods almost immediately, which hurt the investigation further. From then onward, he dumped his victims, wearing little or no clothing, in rivers so that the chance of finding any more fiber evidence was slim. The killings continued, with the murderer claiming more than 20 victims before police began to close in.

Early on the morning of May 22, 1981, a police patrol staking out the Chattahoochee River, where some of the corpses had been found, heard a splash. They rushed to the bridge where the James Jackson Parkway crossed the river and found 23-year-old Wayne Williams, a music promoter, standing there by his station wagon. Williams was questioned and then allowed to leave, but on May 24 the body of 27-year-old Nathaniel Cater was dragged from the river.

When police searched Williams' house and car ten days later, they identified unusual fibers matching those found with the first bodies. But, in order to use them as evidence, they needed to prove that the fibers were not commonly found. After

BELOW Wayne Williams. The match of unusual carpet fibers from his home to those found on his victims' bodies led to his conviction.

further tests, they traced the fibers to a carpet manufacturer in Dalton, Georgia. Over a single 12-month period, the factory had made just 16,397 square yards of carpet using that fiber in the color–"English Olive"–found in Williams' home and car and on the clothes of the victims. Statistics showed that the probability of finding that shade of that particular carpet in any house in Atlanta at the time was one in 7,792.

A second significant fiber was found on the shorts of one of the murder victims and also in the carpeting in Williams' station wagon. The carpet had been made by General Motors, and checks revealed that just 628 out of more than 2.4

ABOVE Police and volunteers searching for clues near the Chattahoochee River.

million cars registered at the time in the Atlanta area were fitted with this type of carpet. That meant the probability of finding this type and color of fiber in any of the other cars was one in 3,828. Furthermore, the probability of another individual having those same carpets in both his or her house and car was almost one in 30 million. Evidence linking the murders was reinforced when similar fibers were found on another ten of the estimated 28 murder victims. Williams was convicted and sentenced to serve two life terms in prison.

hooded attacker

MALCOLM FAIRLEY

A series of burglaries and attacks on households in southern England in 1984 became increasingly violent as the burglar threatened his victims with a shotgun he had stolen from one of his earlier robberies. He eventually began raping his female victims and assaulting their male companions.

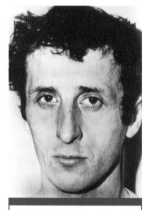

ABOVE Multiple rapist Malcolm Fairley, alias "The Fox."

The man wore a hooded mask, but witnesses were able to report that he spoke with a northern-England accent and was clearly left-handed. On the night of August 17 he stopped on the outskirts of a village called Brampton and decided to strike again, even though he had left his hood at home. He concealed his car in a field and cut a new mask from a pair of green overalls. After walking to the village, he broke into a house, tied up the male occupant and raped his wife. He then casually removed traces of physical evidence, even cutting away a square of bed sheet, and left.

When police searched the area they found valuable pieces of evidence, including tracks that showed where the car had been parked. They also found a

flake of yellow paint where the car had scraped against a tree while being reversed into the hiding place, a leather glove, the burglar's crudely-made mask, and the piece of bed sheet from the victim's home. Nearby, under a covering of leaves, they found the shotgun. Convinced that the suspect would return to retrieve the gun, police mounted a stake-out operation.

The paint sample was analyzed and the color identified as "Harvest Gold." That

ABOVE Armed police officers at Linslade Wood, near Leighton Buzzard, searching for the rapist known as "The Fox."

BELOW The search for "The Fox" extends to a house in the Bedfordshire village of Edlesborough.

BOTTOM LEFT Detective Chief Inspector John Branscombe shows the crudely made hood worn by "The Fox" during his attacks, against a background of other pieces of evidence, including gloves, shotgun cartridges, and a sawn-off shotgun.

color had been used on only one model, an Austin Allegro made between May 1973 and August 1975. Police also searched the national computer for details of burglars from the north of England who were known to have moved south.

The grueling manhunt continued until September, when two officers went to check an address in north London. The resident was one Malcolm Fairley, and officers found him outside washing his car--an Austin Allegro, painted in Harvest Gold. When they questioned him about his recent activities, he gave them evasive answers in a pronounced northern accent. On the back seat of the car was Fairley's watch, which the police asked him to put on. As he complied, they saw that he was left-handed. The car itself bore evidence of damage at a height consistent with the position of the yellow paint flake found on the tree near Brampton. When police searched Fairley's flat, they found two more sets of overalls identical to those used to make the mask. The suspect confessed and on February 26, 1985, Malcolm Fairley was given six life sentences for a series of violent attacks and rapes.

WRITTEN IN BLOOD

An adult has some ten pints of blood circulating around the body, pumped under pressure by the heart. This can mean trouble for a potential attacker. Any cutting or piercing of major blood vessels can produce a flood that will leave significant traces of blood at the crime scene. Such traces can show how a victim was attacked and help identify a multitude of objects associated with the crime. Even the attacker's own blood, shed in a violent struggle, can tie him or her to the scene as surely as a photograph or an eyewitness identification.

Red alert

Bloodstains and splashes can often tell a vivid story. Drops of blood that fall onto a floor or other horizontal surface, for example, show examiners about how far they fell before hitting the surface. This helps them figure out the position of the victim when he or she shed the blood.

If the blood falls only a short distance, the marks are circular or, if the surface is at an angle to the horizontal, the marks are elliptical in shape. If the drops fall a few feet before hitting the surface, the edges of the circular mark are crenellated, that is, they have regular indentations. The degree of crenellation increases proportionately with the length of the fall. If drops fall from a height of six

RIGHT Bloody footprints provide evidence at a crime scene.

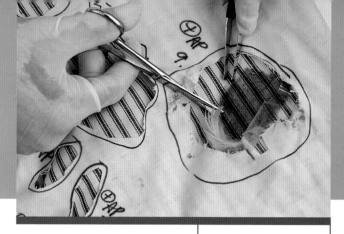

feet or so, there are usually side spurts radiating from the site of the main drop.

Drops of blood shed from a moving source, such as a wounded victim trying to escape, often resemble a stretched exclamation mark: the end of the stain showing the smaller blob indicates the direction of the subject's movement. Stains made by blood spurting under pressure from a major blood vessel show where a serious or even fatal blow was struck. Sometimes blood splashes upward onto a wall or partition, for example. The height reached by spurting blood can show whether the victim was standing, sitting, kneeling or lying down when the blow was struck. Furthermore, the quantity of blood spilled, when compared with the victim's injured body, can be linked with particular wounds. Pools of blood can also show where the victim died, even if the body was later moved.

ABOVE Checking bloodstains on a pillow recovered from a crime scene.

BELOW At the crime scene collecting blood samples for analysis.

Tests for blood

In many cases, blood spilled at a crime scene is all too obvious. But even when criminals have tried to clean up all the evidence, examiners must make sure they locate every remaining trace. The first test simply uses a powerful light. The light's beam, held at an angle over every surface at the scene, can often reveal traces of blood that would otherwise remain unnoticed.

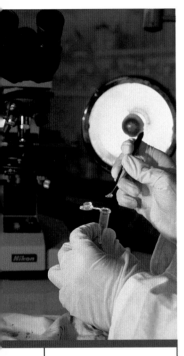

A more powerful test relies on a chemical called luminol, which reacts with blood to produce a faint luminescence. Examiners darken the room being tested and spray all suspect areas with the chemical. All spots and stains of blood then emit a detectable faint blue glow.

Once blood has been collected, another forensic question arises: Is it human? To identify blood as human, analysts place a sample in a test tube above a layer of rabbit serum that has been sensitized to human blood. This serum is specially prepared by injecting a rabbit with human blood, then allowing the appropriate antibodies to form in the animal's bloodstream before extracting a sample. If the blood found at the crime scene is human blood, a cloudy ring will appear at the junction of the suspect sample and the rabbit serum.

ABOVE Forensic scientist places a sample of bloodstained clothing into a sample tube for analysis.

BELOW Photomicrograph of human spermatozoa.

Secretors

Regardless of blood group, around 80 percent of the population qualify as "secretors" because the antigens, antibodies, proteins and enzymes that characterize their blood are also found in other body fluids, such as tears, sweat, saliva, vaginal fluids, and semen. The remaining 20 percent or so of the population carry this information only in the blood. However, in secretors, samples of skin and muscle tissue, and even saliva left by a smoker on the butt of a cigarette can yield much evidence.

Forensic examination is then simplified because a sample of saliva can be quickly and easily obtained once a suspect is identified. Examiners can test the sample and check the results against crime-scene evidence.

Seminal fluid

In cases of rape and other sexual crimes, the seminal fluid the attacker leaves on the victim's body or on clothing or furniture is another powerful source of evidence. Since sperm in the fluid remain alive for only a relatively short time, the condition of the

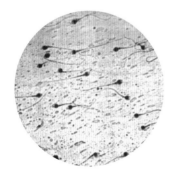

Blood groups

Every detail extracted from a blood sample helps to narrow the field of possible sources. For example, some 46 percent of the U.S. population has type O blood, 42 percent has type A blood, about nine percent has type B, and three percent type AB. An enzyme called phosphoglucomutase 2-1 (PGM2-1) is also found in 36 percent of the population, regardless of blood group. So if PGM2-1 is found in a sample of type A blood, for example, the field of potential sources is narrowed to 0.36 x 0.42 or 15 percent of the population. Examiners use traces or absences of other proteins and enzymes to help single out an individual blood sample.

In some cases, they can narrow the field of possible sources to hundredths of one percent of the population—a degree of accuracy that is highly useful in both eliminating or implicating suspects.

Blood from a shoe is reconstituted in a saline solution before being dropped into a test tube containing different antibodies to determine the blood group.

sample can tell examiners about what time the attack occurred. In the case of secretors, such a sample will reveal the blood group and the presence or absence of other enzymes and proteins that helps to narrow the search for potential subjects. To isolate samples of seminal fluid, examiners use tests similar to those used to reveal the presence of bloodstains.

LEFT A forensic serology laboratory, specializing in testing and analysis of body fluids.

THE DINGO BABY

Michael and Lindy Chamberlain took their two sons, aged six and four, and their nine-week-old daughter Azaria on a camping holiday to the interior of Australia in August 1980. On the evening of August 17, the baby was snugly cocooned in blankets in a baby carrier at the back of the tent where the younger boy was also asleep. Lindy Chamberlain was cooking supper some 60 feet away. Michael Chamberlain claimed he heard a short, sharp cry at around eight o'clock, and Lindy started back to the tent to check the baby.

BACKGROUND Lindy Chamberlain and her husband Michael, a pastor with the Seventh Day Adventist Church, entering the court at Alice Springs in 1982.

OPPOSITE TOP Michael and Lindy Chamberlain with their attorney.

OPPOSITE BOTTOM Lindy Chamberlain pictured in 1986 arriving at court in Darwin to attend the enquiry into her conviction.

Lindy Chamberlain later said that she was astonished to see an Australian wild dog, or dingo, backing out of the tent and shaking something violently in its jaws. The dingo disappeared into the darkness, at which point the horrified Chamberlains found their baby was missing. The alarm was raised and trackers began combing the surrounding countryside. It wasn't until eight days after the baby's disappearance that most of her bloodstained clothes were found. But, curiously, there were no traces of dingo hair or dingo saliva on the garments. Investigators concluded that, since there were no pulled threads on Azaria's clothing or any other signs that a dingo was involved, humans must have attacked the child. The pattern of the bloodstains suggested that the child had been injured by a cut to the throat with a knife rather than by any kind of animal bite. It was also reported that two bloodstained prints of small adult hands were found on the jumpsuit.

Suspicion began to center on the Chamberlains themselves. Bloodstains from a child less than six months old were found in their car on the carpet and around the supports for the front seats. Stains were also found on the blade, handle, and hinges of a pair of scissors inside the vehicle. The couple were tried in September 1982 for the murder of their baby daughter, and though both partners pleaded not

guilty, in October Lindy was convicted of the murder and Michael Chamberlain was convicted as an accessory.

The trial drew continuing controversy, and critics attacked much of the prosecution evidence. The "handprints," for example, were said to be random bloodstains. Other skeptics wondered when and where the Chamberlains would have had the opportunity to kill the baby and dispose of the body on a packed campsite. Two appeals were mounted, but they were unsuccessful and Lindy Chamberlain remained in prison.

In 1986, controversy resurfaced when the baby's missing jacket, now torn and bloodstained, was discovered in a dingo cave near the campsite. In the light of this new evidence, Lindy Chamberlain was released. There was apparently a wealth of evidence in this case, but too much of it was open to more than one interpretation. Ultimately too much evidence remained unexplained to settle the important questions beyond reasonable doubt. In June 1987 the couple were officially pardoned, and in September 1988 their convictions were quashed.

Crime FILE

The bloody message of

GHISLAINE MARCHAL

Ghislaine Marchal was found dead in the cellar of her villa, "La Chamade", in the village of Mougins in the south of France on June 24, 1991. Pierced by a succession of strikes from her killer's knife, she had apparently managed to write on the wall in her own blood as she lay dying. Police read the damning words: "Omar m'a tuer" (Omar killed me) and again "Omar m'a T..."

BELOW Omar Raddad waits for the start of his trial in Nice on January 24, 1994.

The case seemed brutally simple. Her Moroccan gardener, Omar Raddad, was missing from the villa-- as was the sum of 4,000 francs. Raddad was charged with her murder and appeared in court in February 1994. During the trial, the prosecution called in two expert graphologists who certified that the letters written in blood on the wall were consistent with Ghislaine Marchal's own handwriting. For comparison, they used newspapers found in the villa where Marchal had filled in crossword puzzles. It seemed as if the prosecution had established Omar Raddad as the wielder of the fatal knife, and he was sentenced to 18 years in prison.

However, since 1994, an increasing number of doubts have surfaced over the way in which the evidence was collected and presented. Raddad proved a model prisoner and was eventually pardoned by President Jacques Chirac. But he has continued to proclaim his innocence and has taken legal action to appeal the guilty verdict and plead for a retrial.

Unfortunately, the appeals procedure is long and difficult, and it requires new-found evidence that casts doubt on the original verdict. Raddad's lawyer, Jacques Vergès, based his case for an appeal on three grounds. Professor Fournier, a specialist in forensic medicine, testified that the murder had actually been committed on June 24, 1991, a day later than was alleged at the trial. For that day, Raddad had a solid alibi, having spent June 24th with friends and relatives in Toulon. Two different graphology experts, one of them the president of their professional association, found inconsistencies between the letters written in blood and those on the crossword puzzles. They were convinced that the words could not have been written by someone dying from loss of blood. Other experts have denounced the fact that Madame Marchal's fingertips were not measured, to compare with the blood message, and that her body was cremated.

Finally, two private detectives have criticized the police methods and suggested other suspects who might have written the message to incriminate Raddad and conceal their own role in Marchal's death. One pointed out that the murderer's clothing would have been soaked in blood, but the clothes Raddad was wearing at the time of the murder contained no trace of blood. The other noted that a car with two Italian men and a woman had been present at the scene. Also, a pair of rubber gloves which could have been used to write the bloody message had been left in the sink of the villa, then burned in the fireplace along with Ghislaine Marchal's diary. A case that seemed clear-cut because of the evidence now seems more complex than ever because of contradictions revealed by additional forensic evidence.

TOP The bloody message, apparently written by Ghislaine Marchal as she lay dying.

OPPOSITE TOP A smiling Omar Raddad starts his new job in an Islamic Butchery in Marseille on September 14, 1998.

BELOW Omar Raddad leaving Murel's detention center on September 4, 1998.

CHAPTER 12

DNA: THE ULTIMATE IDENTIFIER?

From the earliest days of forensic science, those who track down criminals have longed for some universal identifier, some attribute entirely unique to each individual that would be difficult or impossible to disguise. At last, the answer has been found--and it lies in something more fundamental to the individual than patterns on the surfaces of the fingertips: it lies inside the cells.

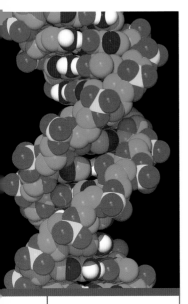

ABOVE Computer graphic image of part of a DNA molecule with the atoms represented as colored spheres: yellow for phosphorus, red for oxygen, green for carbon, blue for nitrogen and white for hydrogen.

Every human body is made up of vast numbers of different types of living cells. Inside every cell nucleus lies a string of coded information in the form of a ribbon-like molecule of deoxyribonucleic acid (DNA) that contains the genetic blueprint of that individual's makeup. Because everyone's genetic make-up is unique, this coded information is as individual as a perfect set of fingerprints with one added advantage to forensic investigators: The information is almost impossible to eliminate. The codes contain a vast amount of information, and the complete human genetic code contains everything from a person's height and build to the color of hair and eyes.

The DNA code

The DNA-coded sequence that specifies a single individual once seemed to be an impossibly long and complex set of instructions. Yet scientists soon realized that, since human beings share many basic characteristics, large stretches of the genetic code must be the same for everyone. The DNA elements that could actually single out an individual were those particular segments responsible for specific details such as physical appearance, family traits and color of eyes or hair.

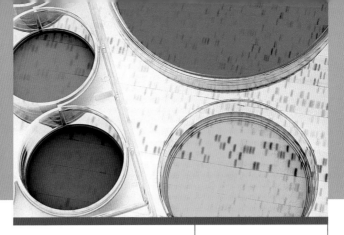

Scientists knew they needed some form of marker that would allow them to isolate these pieces of an individual's DNA code. That way, they could be recorded and eventually compared with corresponding information from other individuals or samples. By the 1980s, a team of genetics researchers at the Lister Institute of the University of Leicester in England, led by Dr. Alec Jeffreys, had found a solution. The researchers isolated particular parts of the DNA code by taking cell nuclei from a sample and using a substance called a restriction enzyme to cut the DNA chain at specific points. The enzyme did this by recognizing a sequence in the code and cutting the chain at specific points to produce a series of fragments of varying lengths. These were then sorted by a technique called gel electrophoresis, which causes the different DNA fragments to move through the gel at different rates. The shorter pieces move faster than the longer ones, effectively sorting the different fragments according to their length. The fragments are then transferred to a special nylon membrane.

ABOVE Dr. (now Sir) Alec Jeffreys working in his laboratory.

Building the "genetic fingerprint"

Scientists then place the nylon sheet containing the DNA fragments on X-ray-sensitive film. A radioactive genetic marker will have bound to those fragments containing the code sequence being studied, and this affects the film at the points where they appear.

Rules of inheritance

Because each newborn child inherits half its chromosomes, together with their DNA, from its parents, any genetic fingerprint from the child's DNA must match up in every detail with the equivalent genetic fingerprint of one parent or the other. The DNA of different children of the same couple has the same relationships with the parents' DNA. This makes it possible to identify individual DNA samples by comparing them with those of known relatives or descendants. In 1991 the Russian government made public the discovery of the remains of Tsar Nicholas II and his family, executed during the Russian Revolution in 1917. In order to identify them, examiners needed DNA samples from the remains, as well as from a direct descendant of a family member. Prince Philip, Duke of Edinburgh and husband of Queen Elizabeth II, who was descended from the Tsarina's sister, provided such a sample. Among the skeletons were those of a man, a woman and their three children. When the DNA samples were compared with those of Prince Philip it became clear that the woman was related to him, and therefore to the Tsarina's sister. DNA testing had positively identified the bones as those of the Imperial family.

ABOVE Prince Philip, Duke of Edinburgh, a direct descendant of the Tsarina's sister.

BELOW A medical expert locking the cases containing the remains of the Tsar and Tsarina and their children.

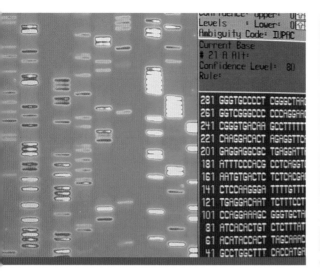

When the resulting plate is developed, it shows the positions of the DNA fragments carrying the radioactive markers.

The DNA fragments appear in a series of bars not unlike the bar codes used to identify different products at a supermarket check-out. The pattern, or the DNA "fingerprint," is unique in every case, except where identical twins or other identical multiple births are involved.

In the future, this powerful technique will become faster and easier to use and will yield even more accurate information. Existing methods of comparing the so-called "barcode" traces on an X-ray film are being replaced by a new technique Dr. Jeffreys developed in 1991. This improved method extends into millions the odds against two individuals having the same DNA information. The information is now processed to yield a digital code of between 50 and 70 numbers. This precise record can be used to distinguish between DNAs from two or more sources found in the same sample, which sometimes occurs in cases of rape or in the aftermath of a struggle. These digital records can also be stored in computer databases and transmitted virtually instantly across the world to be compared with others.

ABOVE LEFT Computer display from an automated method for decoding sequences of base-pairs in fragments of DNA extracted from the chromosomes in human cells–"DNA fingerprinting."

ABOVE Analysis and comparison of DNA fingerprints.

THE DNA LINK –
the conviction of Colin Pitchfork

The rape and murder of 15-year-old schoolgirl Lynda Mann in the village of Narborough in Leicestershire in November 1983 horrified the local community. The only clue left by the killer was his semen.

Because Lynda had been attacked and killed on a secluded footpath, police felt sure that her murderer was a local man. Newspapers appealed for witnesses and police conducted inquiries door-to-door, but no worthwhile leads surfaced.

On July 31, 1986 another 15-year-old, Dawn Ashworth from Enderby, was raped and murdered on another quiet footpath, after having visited friends in Narborough. The DNA evidence proved beyond all doubt that the same unknown man had killed both girls, and the police redoubled their efforts.

With this precise DNA evidence on record, the police turned their attention back to the adult male population of Narborough and the neighboring villages of Littlethorpe and Enderby. But this time

BELOW Removing Lynda Mann's body from the scene.

ABOVE Analyzing the mass **DNA** samples in this case.

ABOVE LEFT Police collecting evidence at the scene of the murder of Lynda Mann.

they went beyond asking questions, they asked for blood samples. In all, more than 4,500 men provided blood samples. According to the paperwork, one of these was Colin Pitchfork, a 27-year-old bakery worker whom police had questioned earlier in the investigation. But on September 18, 1987, a policeman whose father owned a local pub made an interesting report. Bakery workers had been heard discussing the fact that Colin Pitchfork had paid a workmate, Ian Kelly, to give a blood sample on his behalf. Police checked the signature at the blood test against Pitchfork's genuine signature, which appeared on the forms he signed during the original inquiry. The two signatures did not match. Pitchfork was arrested and required to provide a genuine blood sample–one that confirmed he was the double murderer. He confessed to the crime and in January 1988 was imprisoned for life.

THE FUTURE OF FORENSIC SCIENCE

Forensic science is now more powerful than ever before, and it yields information that promises to be increasingly reliable in the future. Because these technological advances can strongly affect people's lives, they raise legitimate concerns about accuracy and civil liberties that also must be addressed.

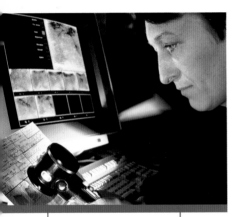

ABOVE Using a hand-held scanner to feed paper fingerprint records into the computer database, where they can be compared side-by-side with suspect prints.

Among these advances are more methods, besides DNA or fingerprint analysis, that can be used to positively identify an individual. They include bar and contour voice prints, retinal scanning, and the analysis of chemicals present in perspiration. In theory, all these different identifiers can be used to build up a database of criminal records that could be cross-matched to check evidence or help identify suspects. They may also be used to screen regular citizens for security purposes.

Crime-busting computers

During the last decades of the 20th century, computers became increasingly useful for law enforcement purposes. In the United Kingdom, the first police national computer was developed during the 1970s to give different forces all over the country access to a common bank of criminal records. In 1987 the British government introduced an additional computer system called the Home Office Large/Major Enquiry System (or HOLMES, after the great fictional detective). Investigation teams could use the computer's pattern-sensing capabilities to suggest potential suspects, or to deliver a list of suspects.

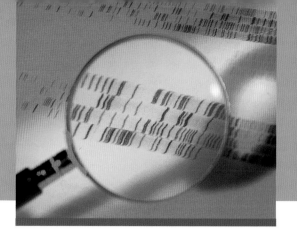

In the United States, the FBI developed an "artificial-intelligence" computer system called "Big Floyd," named for the far-from-fictional Floyd Clark, head of the bureau's Criminal Identification Division. Big Floyd stored more than three million records belonging to the FBI Organized Crime Information System. Operators can use it to interrogate the computer to search for potential suspects. Or, if they have a certain suspect in mind, the computer can reveal all the known information on that person.

Some of the most difficult criminals to identify and track down are serial killers, who often find and strike their victims apparently at random. Between 1979 and 1983 the FBI's Behavioral Sciences Unit developed detailed psychological profiles of known serial killers.

TOP A magnifying glass over two **DNA** sequences. The sequence, also known as an autoradiagram, is four rows of irregularly spaced black bands.

ABOVE A technician using a barcode reader to enter fingerprint details into a computer file.

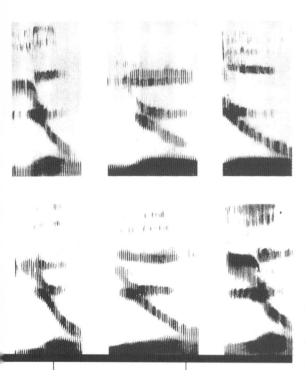

Staff members interviewed more than 20 convicted serial killers and their families and used this information to compile the profiles, which are used to help identify other criminals who show similar behavior patterns. In addition, the Violent Criminal Apprehension Program (VICAP) records details of violent crimes, categorizing the distinguishing features of each attack. Supplied with details of a new case, the program searches its database to find the ten closest matches. Experts then analyze the resulting list to consider whether the most recent crime may be one of a series committed by the same person.

ABOVE Bar voiceprints showing a suspect saying the word "you" at top left. Five individuals repeated the word, and the positive match is shown at bottom right.

Criminal voices

Although some mimics can be quite convincing, the characteristics of a person's voice are also highly individual. Voiceprints are made by recording two and a half seconds of a subject's speech on magnetic tape, then scanning the tape electronically to determine the different frequencies generated in the voice. The results are either displayed on a computer screen or drawn on a rotating drum by a moving stylus.

People with similar voices speaking the same words will still create patterns that are clearly distinct from one another. Moreover, when a person tries to disguise the voice by using an unusually high or low pitch, the pattern may move vertically up or down the display, but it still shows the characteristic pattern. The identity of the speaker will be revealed when the voiceprint is compared with the normal voice recording.

In the United States, voiceprints have been used in several cases to confirm the identity of telephone callers. They can also help identify, for example, a suspect who has made a ransom demand, left a threatening message or made a hoax call. During the early 1990s, tests carried out by the U. S. Air Force Systems Command showed that voiceprint identification was highly reliable. A voice-recognition computer system was used to control access to secure areas, and was found to be 99 percent reliable, even when challenged by professional impersonators.

A picture of evil

In many cases, police have only witness descriptions to go on when searching for a suspect. Even now, some police forces call upon skilled portrait artists who sketch likenesses of a suspect based on their talks with eyewitnesses.

However a more standardized system evolved from the work of Hugh C. McDonald, chief of the civilian division of the Los Angeles Police Department, in 1940. McDonald sketched a series of different kinds of eyes, noses, mouths, hairlines, face shapes and other features on transparent sheets so that the witness could select them to assemble a picture of the suspect. This was the basis of the first Identikit system. The original kit contained 32

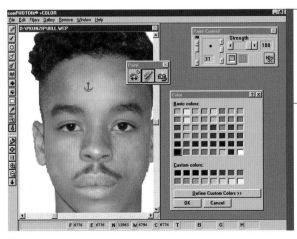

LEFT An Identikit researcher working with a crime victim to compose an image of the criminal's face.

different noses, 33 lips, 102 pairs of eyes, 52 chins and 25 beards and mustaches. Using these elements together with different facial shapes, it was possible to assemble 62 billion different faces.

Since then, computers have played increasingly sophisticated roles in producing and identifying images. Specially designed software enables Photofit (photographically-based) images to be produced in color and in three dimensions to give a more lifelike representation. In addition, faces can be reconstructed from the blurred images retrieved from CCTV (close circuit television) security tapes by using image-enhancement facilities. Computer imagery has also been used–sometimes with great success–in cases where the only physical likeness available is out of date and the image needs to be "aged" to resemble the subject's current appearance.

ABOVE Taking a saliva sample for **DNA** analysis.

TOP LEFT An E-fit composite picture created on computer using a blend of components of individual features from photographs of real people.

OPPOSITE A technician monitoring an analysis by high-performance liquid chromatography (HPLC).

Future possibilities–and pitfalls

Science has advanced to the point that an individual's perspiration can now be tested using chromatography techniques that make the results as unique as a fingerprint. One day, the minuscule traces present in an individual's body odor may be enough to trigger a positive identification. At this time, however, such information is useful only in proving that a known suspect was actually present at the scene where trace evidence was obtained.

These powerful techniques can only assist detectives in finding their suspect in the first place if criminal records are redesigned and expanded to include all relevant information. In some states in the United States, criminals give blood or saliva samples for DNA profiling as a standard part of their post-trial processing. However, it is doubtful this kind of record keeping will be expanded to include the wider public.

The highest scientific standards must be employed at all times to prevent accidental contamination of laboratory equipment, materials, or samples. Slight changes in temperature, small oversights during the testing process, failure to identify the merest trace of a chemical–these kinds of mistakes can cause an array of problems. People working in forensic science must exercise the utmost vigilance in order to protect the innocent while helping to locate, identify, and convict the guilty.

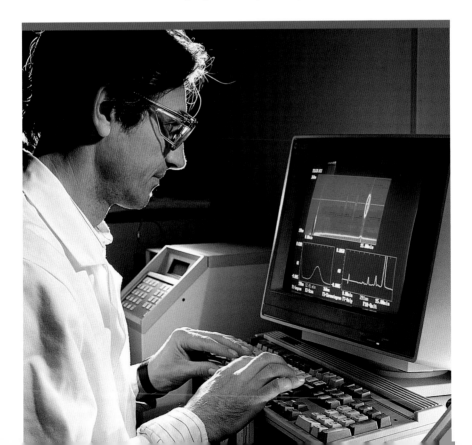

RICHARD RAMIREZ–

out-stalked by a computer

Beginning in June **1984**, a series of **12** violent murders were committed in Los Angeles. In each case, people were attacked in their homes in the middle of the night: male victims were shot, female victims raped. Several of the women were able to describe their attacker, named "The Nightstalker" by newspapers, as a tall, lean Hispanic man with bad teeth and body odor. But this information was not enough to trigger an arrest and the community continued living in fear.

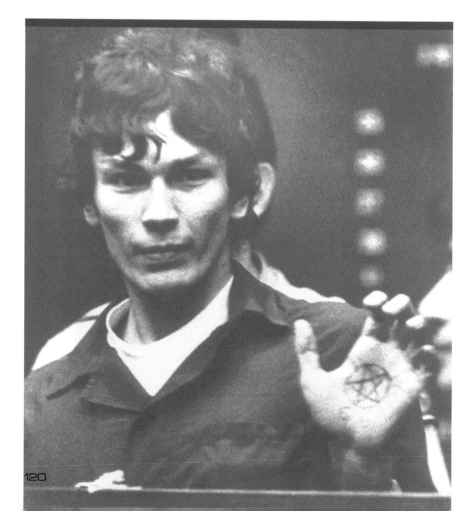

A breakthrough occurred in August 1985 when a victim managed to note the license number of the attacker's car as he drove away. A police hunt located the vehicle, which had been stolen from outside a restaurant on the night of the previous attack. They put the car under surveillance, but the criminal did not return. When forensic examiners searched the vehicle, they turned up a single suspect fingerprint. That one print gave investigators new hope.

Because the Los Angeles Police Department's fingerprint records had been partly computerized earlier that year, police were able to conduct a computer search, which retrieved a positive match. The subject was a Richard Ramirez, who had been fingerprinted following a minor traffic violation some years before. His photograph was circulated to the media, though Ramirez himself, who was out of town, was unaware of it.

On his return, Ramirez visited a liquor store, where bystanders recognized him as the man whose face was printed on the newspapers for sale in the store. As they began chasing him down the streets, Ramirez tried to evade his pursuers but ran headlong into a waiting patrolman, also named Ramirez, and was arrested.

Though Ramirez denied any part in the crimes, it made little difference. Police searching the home of one of his friends had found the gun used in the murders, and jewelry belonging to his victims was found in the possession of Ramirez's sister.

On November 7, 1989, Ramirez was sentenced to death. He might never have been identified but for the computerized fingerprint records and his own date of birth. The computer records only covered criminals born since January 1, 1960, and Ramirez had been born in February of that year.

OPPOSITE Richard Ramirez shows a pentagram on his left palm, a symbol of satanic worship, which had also been found at the scene of two of his crimes.

BELOW Ramirez after his arrest on August 31, 1985–police believe he committed 24 brutal assaults and 16 murders.

O.J. SIMPSON

and the pitfalls of DNA

On June 12, 1994, Nicole Brown Simpson, former wife of football star O.J. Simpson, and her friend Ronald Goldman were found dead just inside the front gate of Mrs. Simpson's home. Both bodies were covered in blood and showed deep knife wounds. Simpson himself was ordered to report to the police, but he fled in a friend's car before eventually returning to give himself up.

ABOVE O.J. Simpson with his ex-wife Nicole Brown Simpson and their children Sidney and Justin.

When Simpson was eventually charged with both murders, it appeared that the forensic evidence against him was so overwhelming that a guilty verdict was inevitable. Some drops of blood found at the scene did not match the blood groups of either of the victims but did have at least three factors in common with Simpson's blood–a trait shared by only one in 200 of the population. DNA profiling carried out on blood drops found on the rear gate of Mrs. Simpson's property showed such a close match with O.J. Simpson's blood that only one person in 57 billion could be expected to produce the same match.

These incriminating drops were found near a set of bloody size 12 footprints that reproduced the sole pattern of a rare design of Bruno Magli shoes. Not only did Simpson wear size 12 shoes, but photographs produced at the later civil trial showed

him wearing shoes of that exact design. When police interviewed Simpson the day after the killings, they also observed a cut on his left hand. A bloodstained left-hand glove was discovered next to the bodies and it bore traces of fibers from Goldman's jeans and shirt; the matching right hand glove, with traces of Simpson's blood, was found at his own home.

Unfortunately for the prosecution, the forensic evidence was largely wasted. Simpson's defense attorneys argued that the police officers involved in the case had a racist bias against their client, and they also cast doubts on the methods used by the forensic laboratories involved who had collected, preserved, and tested the forensic evidence. In addition, they emphasized the absence of a murder weapon and the lack of eyewitness testimony. Certain evidence aided Simpson's defense. Independent witnesses were found who testified they had seen Simpson on the day of the murders. The timing of their sightings indicated that he might not have been at the scene long enough to have committed the killings.

Dr. Henry Lee, director of the Connecticut Forensic Science Laboratory, also appeared to admit under cross-examination that ambiguous blood traces could have been partial shoeprints made by a different sole pattern. If true, this suggested another killer may have been present. Though FBI experts testified that the marks Dr. Lee referred to were not shoeprints at all, the prosecution case had lost credibility, and Simpson was eventually acquitted.

In 1996, the victims' families brought a wrongful death action against Simpson in a civil court and the case was effectively retried. This time Simpson was found responsible for both deaths and ordered to pay huge sums in damages. This second trial appeared to confirm the value of the evidence, but the criminal case remains a powerful reminder that forensic science can only fulfill its purpose when the evidence is collected, analyzed, and presented according to the highest standards.

ABOVE Expert officer Gregory Matheson of the LAPD gave jurors a detailed explanation of the DNA testing methods, earlier believed flawless and foolproof in determining the guilt or innocence of O.J. Simpson.

BACKGROUND Crime scene photograph of the body of Nicole Brown Simpson.

OPPOSITE BELOW Gregory Matheson shows a diagram of six EAP phenotypes to the jury, as part of his explanation of DNA methods.

BELOW Defendant O.J. Simpson wearing the gloves found by Los Angeles police. The prosecutors sought to prove that the gloves fitted Simpson's hands.

Glossary

AFIS: Automated Fingerprint Identification Systems, which enable computers to make rapid and accurate comparisons between new fingerprints obtained at the crime scene and the vast numbers of fingerprints contained in police records.

Agglutination: The tendency of red blood cells to mass together in clumps in reaction to the presence of an antibody.

Antigens: Chemicals which are attached to the surface of the red blood cells to create the different blood groups.

Arches: One of the characteristic patterns of ridges in a fingerprint, possessed by around five percent of the population.

Ballistics: The examination of firearms, the flight of the bullet, and the effects of different kinds of ammunition, in relation to a crime.

Big Floyd: The FBI super computer which contains software, allowing it to search criminal records and analyze the available information in the hunt for those responsible for a particular crime.

Blasting cap: A small explosive charge used to detonate high explosive, which is itself triggered by lighting a safety fuse or applying an electric current.

Blood group: A classification system which divides human blood into groups A, B, AB and O, according to the antibodies and antigens carried by the red blood cells.

Cadaveric spasm: A physical state occurring after an especially violent death, in which the victim continues to tightly clutch any object he or she was holding at the time of death.

Caliber: The internal diameter of the barrel of a firearm, and consequently the diameter of the bullets it fires.

Choke: The constriction of the barrel of a shotgun to reduce the spread of shot as it leaves the gun, to increase its effective range.

Comparison microscope: Two compound microscopes (see below) formed into a single unit, so that objects placed under each objective can be compared side by side in a single eyepiece to reveal differences or similarities.

Compound microscope: The basic microscope which uses two lenses (or combinations of lenses), an objective lens and an eyepiece lens, to focus a greatly magnified image of the subject on the retina of the observer's eye.

Concentric fractures: Patterns of cracks in glass pierced by a bullet, which run between the **Radial fractures** (see page 126) and which originate on the side of the glass from which the impact came.

Delta: A characteristic junction in the looped ridge patterns seen in the fingerprints of approximately 65 percent of people.

Dental records: A standard system for classifying an individual person's teeth according to their distribution, their displacement, and their appearance, together with any gaps or evidence of repairs. This technique is quite useful for identification of bodies because teeth are virtually indestructible.

Depressants: Drugs that depress the action of the central nervous system, for example phenobarbital, pentobarbital and alcohol.

Diatoms: Microscopic algae-like organisms found in lake and river water, which reveal by their presence whether a victim found in these surroundings died by drowning, or was already dead on entering the water.

DNA: Deoxyribonucleic acid, the molecules of which carry the body's genetic blueprint, and which provide a unique identifier for each individual.

Double action: A gun action where the pulling of the trigger to fire a round re-cocks the gun so that the next round is ready to be fired by another pull on the trigger (compare this with **Single action**).

Dry drowning: Death caused by a body reflex from a spasm of the larynx due to the shock of the victim falling into the water, resulting in the heart stopping.

Electron microscope: A microscope that forms its image by the electrons emitted from the specimen when scanned by a focused beam of electrons.

Femur: The thighbone, which can be measured and used to estimate the height of the person to whom it belonged.

Fingertip search: The careful, inch by inch combing of the crime scene by a team of searchers to turn up the smallest items of forensic evidence.

Forensic anthropologist: Specialist who can determine whether or not bones or other remains are human in origin and, if so, reveal details about how the victim died and how they appeared in life.

Forensic chemist: Specialist in the analyses of drugs, dyes, paint samples and other chemicals involved in crimes.

Forensic dentist: Specialist in examining the teeth of murder or accident victims for identification purposes, and for comparison with bite-mark evidence at crime scenes.

Forensic document investigator: Specialist in examining forged documents and forged signatures.

Forensic entomologist: Specialist in the different types of insect life that may be found on corpses or at murder scenes and help to indicate the time, season and weather when a crime may have been committed.

Forensic geologist: Specialist in the characteristics of soil samples, and what these can reveal in terms of the movements of a victim or a suspect.

Forensic pathologist: Specialist pathologist responsible for carrying out autopsies of murder victims and recording of evidence found on or in the body as to the manner and time of death.

Forensic photographer: Specialist who records forensic evidence on film at the crime scene or in the forensic laboratory.

Forensic psychiatrist/psychologist: Experts who evaluate a murder scene and victim to produce a possible psychological profile of the murderer.

Forensic serologist: Specialist in the study of blood and other bodily fluids in addition to DNA for identifying possible suspects.

Gas chromatography: A technique for separating complex mixtures of substances according to their movement when carried by gas through a thin film of liquid.

Gel electrophoresis: A method of testing for human blood by the movement of antibodies and antigens on a gel-coated plate exposed to an electrical field.

Graphology: The science of handwriting analysis, used in forensics to determine a forgery, for example.

Hallucinogens: Drugs like marijuana, LSD, PSP and Ecstasy, which produce changes in mood, thought and perception.

Hemoglobin: A protein in red blood cells that carries oxygen in the blood.

High explosives: Explosives that produce an extremely intense explosive effect when they detonate, and a supersonic pressure wave.

HOLMES: Acronym for the Home Office Large/Major Enquiry System, the UK mainframe police computer system.

Hypothermia: A body temperature that is below normal.

Identikit: The first packaged system for reconstructing the appearance of suspects' faces, based on a wide choice of drawings of facial features.

Latent fingerprints: Fingerprints at a crime scene which are present but cannot be seen until they are made visible through one of several different laboratory techniques.

Liquid chromatography: Technique for separating complex mixtures into their constituents by dissolving the mixture in solution and passing it through a finely divided absorbent material.

Livor mortis: A coloration of the skin of the lower parts of a corpse, caused by the settling of the red blood cells as the blood stops circulating.

Low explosives: Explosives where the detonation is less violent than in high explosives and produces a subsonic pressure wave.

Luminol: A substance which can be sprayed on to furnishings at a crime scene to reveal traces of blood as spots of bright light.

Mass spectrometry: A technique for identifying the constituent parts of a mixture by passing their molecules through a high-vacuum chamber where they acquire a positive charge through colliding with a beam of electrons, which separates them according to their different masses.

Glossary

Mitochondrial DNA: A type of DNA which is found in particular structures of the body and which is passed on intact through the female line of descent.

Narcotics: Drugs which exercise a pain-killing or analgesic effect and which can create a physical dependence among regular users.

Neutron activation analysis: Technique for identifying a substance by bombarding a sample with neutrons in a nuclear reactor, and measuring the energies and intensities of the gamma rays which result.

Nucleotides: The basic building blocks of the DNA helix, each consisting of one of four types of base (adenine, cytosine, guanine or thymine) attached to a sugar-phosphate group.

Plasma: The basic fluid constituent of blood, which carries the different blood cells.

Protein: Polymers made up of amino acids which are the basic building blocks of living organisms.

Pump-action shotgun: A gun carrying several cartridges in an internal magazine, and which can be reloaded by simply pushing a slider backwards and forwards.

Radial: A loop formed as part of a fingerprint pattern which opens towards the thumb.

Radial fractures: Fractures which form a star shape when a sheet of glass is pierced by a bullet, and which originate on the side opposite to the initial impact.

Rigor mortis: The stiffness of the body after death, which helps to determine the time of death.

Sciatic notch: Characteristic shape of part of the hipbone which can indicate whether a skeleton is that of a male or female.

Secretor: An individual who carries his or her blood group information in all their body fluids, including saliva and sweat, for example.

Single action: A type of revolver which needs to be cocked before each shot by pulling back the hammer (see **Double action**).

Stimulants: Drugs which increase the activity of the central nervous system, creating feelings of confidence and energy.

Striations: Fine lines in the internal rifling of a firearm caused by the cutting tool, which impart an individual identity to the gun, and to any bullets fired from it.

Strangulation. The act of suffocating by constricting the windpipe so air cannot enter the lungs.

Suffocation. Death from the lack of oxygen, for example when air is prevented from entering the nose and mouth or pressure on the chest makes breathing impossible.

Tattooing: A characteristic pattern in the skin caused by particles of unburned and partly burned powder from a shotgun blast at very close range.

Tibia: The shin-bone, which can be used as a guide for calculating the a person's height.

Toxicology: The study of poisons, their effects and symptoms and tests to reveal their use.

Ulnar: A loop pattern on a fingerprint which has its open end towards the little finger (as opposed to **Radial**).

Vitreous humor: The fluid which fills the eyeball and which shows changes after death which can be used as an accurate way of identifying the time of death.

Voiceprints. A recording of a subject's speech on magnetic tape which can be scanned electronically to determine the different frequencies generated in the voice, then used to help identify the speaker.

Whorls: Fingerprint patterns where the ridges turn through at least one complete circuit.

X Rays: Electro-magnetic radiation of high energy and very high frequency which can penetrate most materials to different extents and reveal their underlying structure.

Index

Index

Photo Credits

The publisher would like to thank the following for permission to reproduce images. While every effort has been made to ensure this listing is correct, the publisher apologizes for any omissions.

Atlantic Syndication Partners: 39-b. **Black Museum:** 9-t, 11, 18, 21-b, 31-t, 36-t, 37-b, 41, 46, 59-b, 69-t, 95, 116. **Neville Chadwick:** 112/3. **Corbis:** 20, 21-r, 42, 43, 55-t, 58, 64/5, 66-b, 67, 104, 114, 120, 121. **Dr N Daeid:** 69 (b), 70, 88, 89 (b). **Fotomas Index:** 8. **Jonathan Goodman:** 48. **Wilf Gregg:** 26, 27. **Hulton Getty:** 29-b, 80. **Robert Harding:** 52, 54 (b), 68. **International Civil Aviation Organisation, Quebec:** 19. **Oxford Scientific Films:** 16. **Popperfoto:** 27-bg, 76-l, 77, 78, 79, 86, 87, 106, 107, 110, 122-t, 123-b+bg. **Rex Features:** 7-l+r, 14, 15, 28, 30, 31, 36-b, 37-t, 40, 45-b, 49, 59-t, 61-b, 62, 71, 72, 82, 100, 102-b. **Roger Voillet:** 10, 50, 51. **Science Photo Library:** 6-r; Cristina Pedrazzini: 22; Peter Menzel: 1, 13, 103-b, 111-l, 115-t; Dr Jurgen: 2, 102-t; Phillipe Plailly: 12; Tony Craddock: 29-t; John Greim: 32-t; James King-Holmes: 33-t; Manfred Kage: 39-t, 55-b, 91-r; Stephen Dalton: 60/61-t; Robert Holmgren: 81-b; Geoff Tompkinson: 84, 119; Alfred Pasieka: 89-t; Astrid & Hans Friedler: 90; Andrew Syred: 91-t; Michael Viard and Peter Arnold: 103-t, 115-b, 118-l; Profesor Seddon and Dr Evans: 108-t; Robert Longehaye: 109-t; David Parker: 111-r. **Science and Society Picture Library:** 9. **Sirchi Fingerprint Laboratory:** 17, 92, 93, 94, 117. **Solo Syndication:** 38. **Frank Spooner:** 4, 7-m, 23, 25-b, 32-bg, 33-bg, 44, 45-t, 54-t, 56, 57, 60-b , 61-m, 63, 66, 73, 74, 75, , 76-r, 81-t, 83, 85, 91-b, 96, 97, 101, 109-b, 118 -r, 122-b, 123-t. **Topham Picture Point:** 98, 99, 105. Jerry Young: 24-t.